GATHERING VOICES

essays on playback theatre

Edited by Jonathan Fox, M.A.
and Heinrich Dauber, Ph.D.

Tusitala Publishing

Gathering Voices
Essays on Playback Theatre

Tusitala Publishing
137 Hasbrouck Road
New Paltz, NY 12561, USA
914 255 8163

www.playbacknet.org/tusitala

Published in association with
Julius Klinkhardt Verlag, Bad Heilbrunn, Germany

Cover art by Spee

Library of Congress Catalogue Number: 99-70957

ISBN 0-9642350-2-1

Printed in the United States of America
5 4 3 2 1

CONTENTS

Editors' Foreword

The idea for this collection originated in conjunction with a symposium that took place in May 1997, at the University of Kassel, in Kassel, Germany. Upon the initiative of Heinrich Dauber, a professor of education there, the university invited Jonathan Fox as a guest professor, and together they organized the first academic meeting to focus on playback theatre. The event was well attended, spirited, and international. Most of the contributions in Gathering Voices saw first light at the Playback Theatre Symposium, and what did not (the chapters entitled "A Ritual for Our Time" and "Emerging from Silence") had their genesis there. A complete list of all the Symposium presentations can be found in Appendix A in the back of the volume.

You will find articles from thoughtful individuals active in playback theatre from six countries. They write about what most interests them individually in reflecting on their playback work. Yet we see certain common threads. Many authors discuss the importance of trance in the playback theatre kind of improvisation. Another emphasis, paradoxically, is the value of theory, and even research, as a tool for good practice. There is argument, too, within these pages. Is modern society becoming more or less open to bearing witness to truth? Each culture has its taboos, those areas about which it can be dangerous to have discourse. A number of articles in this book raise the question of playback's role in redeeming history. Another feature of Gathering Voices is the series of playback portraits, highlighting six people who practice playback theatre in very different spheres.

Unless otherwise noted, essays were written in English. Many authors refer to actual stories told by tellers during playback events; the names in these narratives have been changed to honor tellers' privacy.

This book, simultaneously published in English and German, would not have come to fruition without the deep collaboration of the editors, whose determination reached across geographical and professional distance. The project is the culmination of a new level of cooperation between playback theatre practitioners and an academic institution, the University of Kassel.

The team in New York, which included Jo Salas as production designer, Sarah Urech as copy editor, Jenn Barresi as general assistant, and Val Wells as proofreader, performed with marvelous dedication and good cheer. We thank Carol Hanisch for the book design and layout, and also thank Inge Schuler and Debra Moskowitz. Finally, we would like to thank all those who made possible and participated in the Playback Theatre Symposium in Kassel, and most especially the students who gave it such life.

Jonathan Fox, New Paltz, NY   *Heinrich Dauber, Immenhausen, Kassel*

What is Playback Theatre?

The best way to describe playback theatre to someone who has never seen it is to paint a picture. Imagine a room with space at one end for a stage. On this stage sit the actors, facing the audience. On stage left sits a musician, surrounded by instruments. On stage right are two chairs. In one sits the "conductor," who will function as a kind of master of ceremonies. The other will be taken by an audience member, who comes to it voluntarily and recounts a personal experience. The conductor asks certain questions, then when the interview is complete, turns the story over to the actors. Music plays for the transition. Then the actors enact the story, using mime, movement, spoken improvisation. Their aim is to capture the essence of the teller's story. After suitable acknowledgment, the teller returns to the audience, and another teller comes forward.

A playback event consists of a series of stories told by audience tellers. It is a process totally spontaneous, made possible by adherence to the ritual. To the question of what happens if no one wishes to come forward, the answer is of course then there can be no playback theatre—but it almost never happens. For the fact is that when people sense an atmosphere of respect, as well as the actors' skill, no matter what their background or culture, they show an eagerness to tell. It makes for compelling theatre. You get a chance to watch your neighbor's story. Often it touches some vital aspect of your own.

Thus playback theatre is about stories (sometimes called scenes), by which we mean an experience of any sort recounted by the teller and dramatized by the actors. Playback performing companies also utilize a number of short forms, including the dance-like fluid sculptures and the dyadic pairs. In performance a playback company (actors, musician, conductor) will play for an audience, but playback theatre also often takes the form of a workshop, in which a leader/conductor alone facilitates a group to act as well as tell.

INTRODUCTION

Jonathan Fox

As well as serving as the co-editor of this collection, I am also the one who first conceived the playback idea. So I have been intimately involved with playback theatre from the start. It is true that for a few brief moments, the concept resided only with me. But very quickly, playback theatre began to involve others, first Jo Salas, my partner in life and work, then the original playback theatre company, then beyond.

It would be foolish, therefore, for me to try to write any sort of dispassionate account of what playback has accomplished. That must be left to more professional and distanced observers. Rather it seems more fruitful to write a personal history, expressing my own understanding as of approximately twenty-four years after that day when I sat in a café, drank a cup of chocolate, and it came to me, the idea of my dreams.

Historical Development

It was in 1973, once again in the United States after years overseas, that I had discovered my metier in the theatre. It was theatre of a very particular kind—without scripts, personal, informal. I directed groups in enactments. I worked eagerly with all sorts of groups, including very young children, the handicapped, the elderly, and people on the street. The iconoclasm and anti-elitism fueling the experimental theatre movement fueled me, too. I believed in an immediate theatre. I believed in a theatre that could take place everywhere. I believed in a theatre for any and everybody. These experiments culminated in a theatre company called *It's All Grace*, which performed improvisationally developed pieces in outdoor settings.

But my search was not complete. From my university study in oral epics I knew that stories in preliterate societies were always more than mere entertainment: they contained the knowledge of the tribe, both historical and ethical. If we could only get hold of *that*, I thought.

In 1973 I attended a psychodrama in Beacon, New York, and saw Zerka Moreno in action. She also spoke about J.L. Moreno's Stegreiftheater in Vienna. What I heard from her lips, and what I witnessed under her guidance, felt like a revelation. Here was a true community theatre. Here was theatre that made a difference. Here was emotion. Here was often stunning beauty.

Some months later my café vision came to me of townspeople gathering to watch fellow citizens act out their real stories. In its espousal of modern populist ethos, dramatic improvisation, and the ancient oral tradition, this was the idea I had been waiting for.

A year and a half later, playback theatre was born. I had decided to use psychodrama networks to find actors for this new experiment because I felt they might have the requisite spontaneity and empathy. We rehearsed one evening a week and one Sunday a month. Our first performance was for family and friends, the second on a children's hospital ward, the third at an academic conference. At each we came on stage with nothing but our readiness to enact the thoughts, feelings, memories, and experiences of whoever wanted to tell.

Our first five years of practice and performance enabled us to learn that indeed people's everyday concerns could be dramatized with power. As our skill in the form increased, people also shared some of their extraordinary stories. We developed some of the short forms now standard in playback theatre today, such as fluid sculptures and pairs. We learned to appreciate the place of music in our enactments.

We also sought consciously to perform for as many different kinds of audiences as we could. In addition to the general public, these included schoolchildren of all ages, prisoners, the elderly, and the emotionally disturbed. I remember thinking at the time that it was good to be able to bring theatre to people who might never otherwise experience it.

What we felt but could not in those early years articulate was the deep satisfaction of enabling these peoples' stories to be heard, first by the tellers themselves, then by their peers, their helpers, and not least by us. Despite many imperfect performance experiences, our motivation steadily grew, because we responded to the popular wisdom voiced in these stories and the healing power of empathy.

I tried to bring our work to the attention of critics. I tried to obtain funding from governmental arts bodies on the state and national level, as well as from foundations. But these attempts failed. It seemed that playback theatre did not fit in the category of art, or look enough like theatre ("What is the title of your show?" asked one prospective reviewer. "Send me the script. I need to read the script beforehand," said another). In the end, I gave up trying to convince the establishment that playback theatre was of interest as avant-garde theatre.

Playback theatre was indeed beyond traditional funding categories. It did cross the boundaries of art, psychology, and education. In retrospect, this was a source of its strength, and my own needs for artistic recognition were insignificant by comparison.

Furthermore, while I did not achieve my goal of having playback theatre recognized, other objectives were eminently satisfied—I had found a way to express my own theatrical creativity with colleagues and friends; to reinforce playfulness and joy in children (and help adults rediscover these innate qualities); to establish a setting where anyone, even the most marginalized, could tell their story and have it not only listened to, but *heard.*

In 1980 a team of four from the original company was invited to teach in four cities in Australia and New Zealand. In each location we performed with selected participants from our workshops, empowering groups to carry on after we had gone. The next year Mary Good from Melbourne spent a month in New York training and observing our work. The result was a flowering of new playback performing companies—in Sydney, 1980; Melbourne, 1981; Auckland, Wellington, and Perth, 1982; Christchurch, 1984.

In 1986 Annette Henne from Switzerland came to study; she would start PT Schweiz two years later. Christina Hagelthorn had previously attended early PT performances while studying psychodrama in the United States and had brought the work back to her native Sweden.

I was invited to Japan for the first time in 1984. In subsequent years companies started in England, Germany, Russia, Hungary, Finland, Italy, France, Argentina, and Brazil. And so it goes.

At present, Asia is the locus for new activity, including Hong Kong and India. As I write, playback teachers from Australia and New Zealand are also conducting major workshops in Fiji and Kiribati.

In 1986 the original company retired. By then other companies had started to spring up in different communities in North America—in Washington, DC, Boston, Seattle, Pittsburgh, Toronto, Canada, Albany, NY, Newport, RI, and San Francisco. By now many others have joined them.

Christina Hagelthorn created an international playback group in 1990, which performed annually in a different European city. This model was adopted by Deborah Pearson and Robyn Weir, who organized an international women's team to perform at the 1995 Beijing Forum on Women, bringing playback to a new level of attention.

Some of these groups have close ties to psychodrama and some do not, depending on the background of the founders. Because playback theatre is an approach that places considerable emphasis on process and is so totally spontaneous, however, even the unpsychologically-oriented are likely to develop some familiarity with psychodrama as useful learning for their playback practice.

Two factors stimulating the growth of playback theatre have been training and international gatherings. Annual summer courses taught by colleagues, Jo Salas, and myself in New York State grew into the School of Playback Theatre. Currently, a five-week session of courses takes place every July at Vassar College in New York, with additional courses offered throughout the year in other American locations, Europe, and Japan.

Since 1991 when one Swede came to a gathering of Australian/New Zealand playbackers in Melbourne, international conferences have taken place roughly every year and a half—in Sydney, Australia; Rautalampi, Finland; Olympia, Washington (USA); Perth, Australia; and in 1999, in York, England.

In 1990, I joined Jo Salas, Judy Swallow and seven others from around the globe in establishing the International Playback Theatre Network (IPTN), whose purpose was to facilitate communication between playback practitioners and guide the playback movement.

Even though growth has led to a certain level of formal organization, the ties are kept loose. There remains more emphasis on freedom than control. From the outset, we have encouraged individuals from all kinds of personal and professional backgrounds to try out the playback idea in their contexts. Furthermore, the artistic component of playback theatre defies legislation. Thus for ideological and pragmatic reasons, there is no license or certification for the practice of playback theatre.

At the same time, with experience we have learned that playback theatre can command great power. This power can be utilized for good or ill. Undertaking a playback event takes an unusual collection of skills—thus the need for training. (Playback theatre is the kind of endeavor where those who have ten years of experience behind them still talk about how much they need to learn.) We continue to encourage folk to go back home and try out the idea, but we now expect that as they get serious about continuing with playback theatre, they will apprentice themselves to the elders.

After almost 25 years, playback theatre is practiced in about 30 countries. My vision is marvelously fulfilled. In more than two hundred locations citizen actors are acting out the stories of their communities. A body of knowledge has been developed about the practice of playback theatre in different settings. It seems to me that the period of early experimentation is completed, and it is now time to consolidate what we have learned. The 1997 Symposium in Kassel, documented in this publication, is a beginning step in that direction.

How PT is Used

What are the contexts in which playback theatre is practiced? In this section I will describe some of them. The variety of settings is made possible by the flexibility of the totally improvisational PT form, which can vary with regard to duration, number of actors, and workshop or performance format.

PT as community-based theatre. The original company performed on a box-office basis the first Friday of every month, and this pattern of monthly public performances has been perpetuated widely.

PT in education. From the outset, playback has been performed in schools, providing children with validation of feelings and play. Playback school events have also been tailored to curriculum materials. Current trends include expansion at the university level, with the start-up of student companies and the inclusion of PT in the curriculum. There are also signs that as well as an object of study in its own right, the playback approach may be developed as a pedagogical tool.

PT as social service. Playback teams have worked widely in the social service field, often creating workshops where participants are invited to act in each others' stories. Among other things, these sessions teach listening and communication skills.

PT as marker of transition. Playback teams are used as part of orientations, terminations, annual conferences, and similar events to provide a way for a group to share feelings about change.

PT in organizational development. Most often playback is utilized to help trainees integrate their emotional with their cognitive responses. Playback is also used to model and teach teamwork, as well as to raise consciousness about specific issues, such as diversity and corporate culture.

PT in therapy. Playback theatre is often perceived by clients as non-threatening, since they are invited to tell *any* moment, no matter how small or apparently unimportant (in contrast to psychodrama and other methods, which tend toward emphasizing what are perceived as major problems). Playback is also effective as role training, where the emphasis is placed on clients as actors.

Theoretical Foundations

My first identity in playback was as an artist and member of the American experimental theatre. To this end I read voraciously books by the movement's theorists, Artaud and Grotowski, and managed to take workshops with many of its leading lights on the American scene, such as Richard Schechner and André Gregory.

To this I added my study of story—in particular preliterary story (I had written my undergraduate thesis on a 13th century English poem, *Havelock the Dane*). Two years of living in a village in Nepal gave me firsthand knowledge of preindustrial culture.

Although I did not consciously understand it early in the playback years, I was also seeking to embody a transformational ritual that could be a source for hope without whitewashing what is wrong with the world. As a theoretical support for this interest, I turned to the religious existentialists, including Tillich, Buber, and Moreno. (Heinrich Dauber in his *Songlines* article in this book writes about these and other influences.)

What has inspired my playback work lately has been to investigate the relationship between the personal story enacted in a social setting and the "stories" of the culture, including its history. My hope is that the playback ritual could play a part in healing some of the injustices and upheavals of the past that fester not only in individuals, but in whole societies. Thus my playback concerns are very different now than they were twenty-four years ago. Then I thought about solutions to acting problems. I thought about lighting and stage arrangement. I thought about finding an audience. Now I think about those stories that are untold and untellable and finding a trustworthy context for airing them.

Underlying my playback work from the outset has been a commitment to process. This means creating an atmosphere suitable to share our own stories prior to asking audiences to share theirs; this means striving for a genuinely positive group life as well as enchanting audiences. I always wanted a theatre that was good for the actors.

Playback is a collective activity, and inevitably its development has been shaped by many beside myself. I can only mention a few here. First on the list are fellow members of the original company. Jo Salas, a classically-trained violinist originally from New Zealand, influenced the form by her strong aesthetic sense and the nonspecialist ethos that she brought to our work, in which, in a kind of pioneer spirit, anyone might unload the equipment, sew up a shoe, prepare the refreshments, or act in a scene.

Judy Swallow brought a Rogerian value of acceptance and mutual respect that helped deepen our sense of the centrality of empathy in playback work.

Michael Clemente, who died of AIDS in 1992, encouraged us never to lose sight of the underclasses. He also modeled an inspiring level of acting.

Each new playback pioneer brought their own genius and background to the movement. This was especially true when playback theatre began to expand in different countries. Australian and New Zealand practitioners were inspired by (and many actually studied at) the Drama Action Centre (DAC) in Sydney, a school for Commedia dell'Arte, clowning, and community-based theatre. Bridget Brandon and Francis Batten, who was trained in Paris by Jacques Lecoq, founded DAC. Mary Good, a psychotherapist and founder of Melbourne Playback Theatre, was one of their students. Bev Hosking, founder of Wellington Playback Theatre, and now an influential trainer, was another.

The playback theatre practitioners in Europe have been heavily influenced by a background in psychodrama. Christina Hagelthorn from Sweden, Annette Henne from Switzerland, and participants in Hungary, Finland, Italy, and Russia have all discovered playback via this route. This is also true of the nascent playback theatre movement in South America.

The playback movement in Japan has grown within private sector trainer networks. In the mix of eastern and western influences that underlies the response of the Japanese to playback theatre, it remains to be seen what will emerge as its underlying theoretical foundations. As Kayo Munakata, one of the Japanese playback pioneers, has suggested, playback, with its emphasis on warmth and understanding, may recapture a sense of *amae,* or communal fellow feeling, that was the basis of traditional Japanese culture.

The new blossoming of playback in India and Southeast Asia draws on a strong connection to people's theatre influenced by Augusto Boal and the Philippine Educational Theatre Association.

Playback companies from different cultural and theoretical orientations are likely to approach the "zone of good playback" (see "'Good Playback'" and "Ritual" essays below) from different directions. Frequently a group overbalances towards artistic or social values. It turns out that while "good playback" can take place under many different conditions, to achieve it is a considerable challenge. We are still learning what it takes.

The playback movement, as exemplified in the operation of its network and its conferences, places a high value on cooperation and simplicity. Correspondingly, personal profit and aggrandizement are disparaged. The benefit has been a body of practitioners with a commitment to collegial connection and respect for the emergent playback tradition.

This book will offer playback practitioners and other interested readers a sense of the current state of playback theatre. It will also point the way to new ideas that extend well beyond the reach of its inventors, including myself. This is as it should be. For while the growth of the playback idea has naturally been gratifying, what remains most important is the hope that our discoveries will increase the possibility for persons, every sort of person, to have their story heard.

What is "Good" Playback Theatre?

Jo Salas

As guest conductor, I took part in a performance with London Playback Theatre at a weekend celebration held in support of the Beijing Women's Conference. About 80 people crowded into the performance space, an oddly shaped room upstairs at the Royal Festival Hall. The audience was very diverse: women attending the weekend festival, individuals and families who had come especially to see playback, some elderly couples strolling by the Thames who wandered in out of curiosity. I had been warned that British audiences were not easy to engage, so I was relieved when they responded as fully as any other audience. Within minutes strong feelings had been expressed and enacted, people were laughing and crying, and the actors, musician and I were working smoothly together in spite of our unfamiliarity with each other. As the show went on there were some inspired moments of acting, as well as occasional awkwardness or confusion. At the end of the show the applause was warm. People lingered talking to us and to each other before dispersing into the afternoon.

The other performers and I came together before we too went our separate ways. Most of them shared my feeling that it had gone well. But one young woman was in tears of frustration. "I *hated* it!" she said. She felt that the actors had missed opportunities to be as sophisticated as they could be, and, particularly, that she had failed to show the scope of her own skill.

How to account for the radical difference in our perception? My judgment of success was based on my feeling that the performers, myself included, had achieved an acceptable level of performance. Our scenes and so on had been generally well-shaped, and accurate in embodying the essence of the teller's experience. The audience had participated fully from the outset, in spite of the diversity of background, age, ideology, and contact with playback. The familiar phenomenon of audience members lingering afterwards, connected to each other as they had not been before, was another sign to me that what we had done had succeeded.

But for Chloë, the unhappy actor, the audience's satisfaction meant nothing. She hadn't even noticed it. She had been focused on artistic issues to the complete exclusion of the show as a social event. To her, success was something that happened only on stage, not in the room as a whole.

Playback theatre is theatre, and theatre is art. Playback is theatre not simply because that is how it has been named, but because what we do in playback fulfills the very essence of theatre's intention: to convey human experience by enacting it in distilled form; to embody narrative and meaning in the realm of space and time.

It is also an interactive social process with the purpose of service to its audience, a purpose that most other kinds of theatre do not share.

Since playback's earliest days, questions relating to aesthetics and to artistic standards have raised themselves constantly. Can this really be theatre if it is also service? Are we doing it well enough? Can we expect to be acknowledged by others as theatre artists? How can we recognize and measure success in playback? How can we refine it? What do we mean by "good" playback?

What we do is art, but not only art, and maybe not always art. Playback's effectiveness involves artistic excellence—but artistic excellence alone does not ensure success, and further, playback theatre can, in certain circumstances, be fulfilled by people lacking artistic sensibility, skill, or experience.

Evaluating Art

All art is the manifestation of the artist's impulse to create, which itself is an urge to synthesize and to reveal. Art is the revelation of meaning—not the simple depiction of beauty or obedience to laws of form, but the artist's inspired attempt to convey her or his perception of a meaning that emerges from or underlies the randomness of common experience. For the perceiver of art, there is a sense of recognition, delight, a confirmation of truth. The philosopher Newton speaks of the artist's task as being not to create beauty where none existed, but in fact "to lift a corner of the veil and *reveal* beauty:" and by beauty, he means rightness of form and design, not necessarily harmony. Gregory Bateson discusses art in terms of pattern, meaning the presence of elements that repeat in a connected design, so that if you see one part of a pattern you also learn about the other, unseen part. The internal metaphors of a work of art contain information about wider realms—the unconscious, or the nature of reality itself—that are not directly perceivable. The artist's deliberate placement of one element in relation to another matches or illuminates the perceiver's intuition of truth: it is the fact of this relatedness, says Bateson, that is the true subject of art.

Art has the capacity to imply the presence of design, of pattern, as a feature of reality. It can affirm an ontological meaning, which is the knowledge that *being* itself is purposeful. When we raise the question of assessment of a work of art—"how good is it?"—it is this function of affirming meaning that we are asking about. As human beings, we need the affirmation that art gives us, and we want it in strong measure.[1] We need art in order to integrate and comprehend our experience. We are disappointed, even dismayed, by inferior art. We may travel long distances and pay large amounts of money to experience "good" art. If we are artists ourselves we invest enormous effort, usually unpaid, in making our art as fine as we can possibly make it. And as artists, we are not content with anything less than an evaluative aesthetic judgment. We are pleased to know someone has enjoyed our creation; but there is a world of difference between hearing "I enjoyed it" and "This is very good." The pronouncement of value indicates the perceiver's "yes!"—that inward recognition of meaning and truth. It indicates that the artist has succeeded, at least to some degree, in his profoundest task of lifting a corner of the veil and revealing a part of the connecting pattern that lies underneath. The creator of the world itself, according to Genesis, pronounced his work to be good when it was completed, an expression of satisfaction recognizable by any artist.

How do ordinary people, not professional critics, evaluate the art that we encounter? What is it that leads us to perceive something as good art?

Do the music, literature, art and performance that most strongly move and inspire us have anything in common?

There are elements, I believe, shared by all art that is widely recognized as being great. Whether the work is visual, written or performed, these elements include order (in the sense of purposeful design), an integrity of form with some kind of internal cohesiveness, the presence of originality, a high degree of skill in execution, evidence of conviction and inspiration on the part of the artist, and the ineffable sense that the work of art speaks of a reality beyond its own scale.

If an artistic creation possesses all these qualities in abundance, it is likely to be considered by most people as great art. It will create in its audience the strongest experience of revelation of meaning. In the absence of these qualities, or of some of them, a work of art is less likely to generate a consensus of value: its impact will vary from one perceiver to another. But art that is less than great may still fulfill art's deepest purpose for some people. It is perfectly possible for an audience member to be riveted and transported by an amateur concert even if the performers lack the skill of professionals. It depends on the presence of other elements, not exclusively aesthetic: more about this later.

Evaluating Interactive Social Events

As I said earlier, playback theatre is an art, and therefore subject to assessment according to the presence or absence of the elements mentioned above. However, it is more than art: a playback event is also integrally an interactive social event, and subject to success or failure as such. (It is significant that there is no obvious term to refer to the realm of our work that lies beyond pure art. The absence of a familiar or fully adequate term reflects the common difficulty in comprehending and discussing what I am referring to as the "interactive social" domain.)

We live our lives in proximity to others. The groups in which we find ourselves as children—family, neighborhood, and school—may be nurturing, or inadequate, or destructive. With maturity comes the desire to choose, to the degree possible, the nature and quality of the groups that form our social world, the people we live and work with, the groups we learn and play with.

Although most people seek out groups that are rewarding and try to avoid those that are disappointing or harmful, they are not necessarily aware of the components of successful interactive events, and therefore may not be able to consistently choose, build or maintain groups that are truly satisfying and effective. You may notice that your evening language classes run smoothly and feel enjoyable while meetings with colleagues at work leave you dissatisfied or diminished, without realizing that the difference between them is no accident. As in the domain of art, there are distinct elements that are likely to lead to fulfillment, whether in an ongoing group or in a one-time event.

Consider a family gathering, a class, or a town meeting. Although each has its own particular demands, they also share common criteria of success. These include planning and organization according to the purpose of the gathering; a congenial and appropriate physical environment; an opportunity early in the proceedings for each person to be seen and heard; an atmosphere of respect; some form of participation or engagement from all present; the acknowledgment and inclusion of diverse concerns, points of view, and feelings; time management; a sense of achievement in relation to the meeting's intent; and an adequate closure at the end. The more these elements are present, the more the event will be experienced as successful. In their absence, an event is felt to be a failure. Participants are likely to feel disappointed, excluded, frustrated, bored, or left wanting, depending on which aspects were inadequate. A family gathering in which some members sit silent while others laugh and chat will not be successful in bringing the family together; a town meeting that is unplanned will not make progress toward its purpose; a classroom that is too cold or crowded will not be conducive to good learning.

Moreno's method of sociometry addresses particularly the questions relating to inclusiveness and participation. He considered that in any group there is an intricately evolving pattern of relationships between members, resulting in a greater or lesser degree of inclusion and contributing therefore to the group's vitality and effectiveness. Sociometry explores this system of interconnections, with the goal of maximizing and enlivening the participation of all those present.

Groups of many different kinds—vocational, recreational, geographical—are often referred to as "communities," a word rather wistfully overused in our post-industrial era where it is common for people not to know the names of their neighbors. What does "community" mean? It is, I think, the idea of a group of people who acknowledge, value, and maintain their connectedness and their commonality. Jean Vanier, who founded a series of group homes for disabled people in France, described community as "a group of people who are yearning to bring each other forth."

The qualities that might actually lead to the creation of this kind of community are similar to those I have suggested as necessary to a successful interactive social event: the attention to inclusiveness, the care taken with environment and structure, the matching of design to purpose. Whether in an ongoing situation or within one particular event, fulfillment of these criteria can create community in Vanier's sense—a gathering of people who seek to know each other, to listen to each other, to remember and care for each other.

A Meeting Place

A playback theatre event is integrally both an artistic event and an interactive social event involving both complex group dynamics and sensitive one-to-one communication. If the task of art is the creation of form to express the artist's perception of meaning, then the playback artist's task, specifically, is to create cohesive and shapely pieces of theatre based on an acute sense of the meaning of the teller's story. It is their artist's sensibility that enables playback performers to transform moments from real lives, however simply or roughly told, into well-crafted dramas that have resonance for the audience as well as for the teller. Drawing on their aesthetic sense of story, as well as language, metaphor, and stagecraft, they create art, embodying a pattern of elements in relation to each other in such a way as to suggest the wisdom contained in a larger reality. For the audience, watching and listening is an aesthetic experience—in other words, an experience of affirmation, expansion, revelation, and delight.

This art is different from an art that only seeks to convey the artist's vision: it is an art that is committed to affirming ordinary people's experience and to fostering connections between them so that the communities we live in can grow in compassion and humanity. We strive to hone our art in order to offer it as service. Playback is a fusion, perhaps a unique one, of artistic and social phenomena. The more it can fulfill the demands of both, the more it can succeed.

Every playback practitioner is familiar with the experience of frustration and chagrin when the process seems to fail, and with the elation that can come when it works. The assessment depends somewhat on whether you are considering a whole show or a single scene, whether it is a performance or an applied context such as a therapy or training group, whether you are a performer, a teller, or an audience member, and so on. However, I believe that the criteria I've proposed for success in art and interactive social events will consistently apply, along with some further qualities specific to playback.

Here are two more moments from my own experience when the question of success or failure has been notable for one reason or another:

Four of us from my company, Hudson River Playback Theatre, went to perform as part of a college symposium on reproductive rights. It was several hours' drive from our home. We got there to find that the preparation for our show had been minimal. The location was the corner of a large open space with people wandering through on their way somewhere else. Very few people came for the show. We began by making personal statements relating to the theme, feeling more exposed doing this than if there had been a large audience. One of the organizers told a moving and very disturbing story about an abortion she had had many years ago. The actors enacted it with passion and ingenuity. After it was over, the audience was silent. No-one else wanted to tell anything. We continued as best we could, hoping to somewhat redeem the situation with the strong ending that we had planned. But shortly before the scheduled close our host jumped up and said she was sorry, she'd made a mistake about the time frame and we had to end immediately. It felt very abrupt. In spite of expressions of gratitude from some of the people who were there, we felt that our show had been a failure.

Looking back at our choices that day, I think that we failed, and I especially as the conductor, to create a safe enough space for this tiny audience who had come to explore an extremely delicate topic. Daunted by the inhospitable room and the small turn-out after our long drive, we didn't sufficiently adapt our plan to the situation we found. Our own discomfort as we made our personal statements at the beginning should have warned us that the audience would probably feel similarly exposed. If we had built a better connection with them at the outset, perhaps they would have been willing to journey with us from one story to the next. But the actor's stagework, although skillful and sophisticated, could not by itself draw the audience into more participation. It was in the social domain, not the artistic, that this performance was lacking.

Another moment:

At the Playback Theatre conference in Finland in 1993 there were performances by a number of different groups. A few were companies who had come with all or most of their members, but most were ad hoc groups composed of representatives usually from companies with a common language, if not a common country. All the performances showed a knowledge of playback forms, and some were more accomplished than others, but none fully embodied the playback spirit, in my view, until the last day, when a pick-up group of New Zealanders, Australians, and Hungarians took the stage. They had recognized in each other a kind of anarchic energy and wanted to play together, although they shared neither language nor playback style. Their performance was a great reassurance to me: I had been wondering unhappily what was missing from all the others (all the more troubling to me since four of the groups had asked me to perform with them as a musician). Looking back on it from the perspective of a few years, I recall a joyful interactive creativity among the actors, which made up for the complete absence of actorly polish; and a no-holds-barred attitude to the audience from the conductor. She faced us as though we were a many-headed organism, which we were, and teased, provoked, and cajoled us to tell our stories, not necessarily the ones we thought we wanted to tell. The large audience came alive and felt like a group for the first time in the entire conference.

Acting and Other Playback Criteria

The degree of success of the three performances I've mentioned (London, New York, and Finland) can be accounted for in a general way by the presence or absence of the qualities that I listed earlier as criteria for value in art—artistic form, skill and inspiration, etc; and in social events—skillful attention to inclusiveness, environment and structure, etc. There are also elements that are specific to playback theatre, some that are clearly in the realm of art, others that are simultaneously questions of art and non-art.

In a public performance, the audience wants, expects, and deserves an aesthetic experience. How do we, the playback artists, ensure that they get it?

Like any other artists, playback performers strive to find form in which to embody meaning. The primary artistic task in playback is the transformation of personal stories into theatre pieces, works of art with integrity of form and design. In our work, the meaning we seek to convey is the meaning embedded in the teller's experience.

The tools with which playback performers (including musician and conductor) make such transformations are those of the stage, beginning with aesthetic concerns like the visual set-up. Most importantly, there is the quality of the actors' performance. Good actors use movement freely and creatively. They know how to move and position themselves on stage in order to embody the story and to create an aesthetic, evocative stage picture at every moment. They use language with accuracy, economy and gracefulness. During scenes, they make imaginative and judicious use of the boxes and cloth props. There is a co-creative give-and-take between actors and musician. They have mastered the different demands of specific forms—fluid sculptures, pairs, etc. The ritual framing of the show and each segment within it is fulfilled with presence and dignity.

The quality of acting itself goes beyond the specific use of movement, voice, etc. Playback theatre requires a particular kind of acting which we can call *authentic* acting, as opposed to the more stylized acting familiar from television, film and most other kinds of theatre, however naturalistic. In playback acting, the actor does not use a code to depict emotion but draws her portrayal directly from her sense of the teller and his story.

At its best, this kind of acting can be as powerful and inspired as that of great traditional actors, whose genius is precisely their quality of authenticity built on prodigious skill and training. However, formal theatre training may not be a good preparation for playback acting. Traditional actors are used to basing their performance on a script, not an empathic sense of an actual, present human being, and their technique may distance them from teller, audience, and fellow performers. They may also find it challenging to summon the generosity that playback actors need: part of Chloë's difficulty in the London performance was her concern to make an impression as an "actress" rather than a sense of service to the audience.

Experienced playback actors use a high degree of artistic awareness and skill in their acting: authentic acting does not mean that it is unmediated by an aesthetic consciousness. But because authenticity is the key, it is sometimes possible for completely inexperienced actors to produce very good acting drawing on nothing but empathy and spontaneity. On the other hand, people with a little experience—enough to have lost their beginner's innocence, but not enough to have acquired artistic skill—sometimes fall into serious mistakes in their acting. The problems are often in their attempts to depict story or emotion nonliterally—brandishing a piece of red cloth to show anger, for example, or following the teller's actor around the stage in a clumsy attempt to "be" his inner self. Brand-new actors in their innocence do not think of being anything but literal, while sophisticated actors know how to move fluently and clearly between literal and symbolic action on stage.

The music in playback is another area where artistry is key. Again, spontaneity and empathy on the musician's part can go a long way toward making up for a lack of musical talent or training. But the aesthetic quality of a performance will be greatly enhanced by music that is expertly and sensitively played.

In addition to these artistic considerations, there are elements indivisibly in the realms both of art and of social interaction, and equally essential to playback's success. There is the faithfulness of the enactment to the teller's story, which depends on attentive and empathetic listening on the part of conductor, actors and musician. There is the co-creativity between actors, between actor and musician, between the conductor and the rest of the team. This includes the elusive quality of improvisation itself, which operates on a constant reciprocity of offers, in turn deriving from the performers' sense of the story and where it needs to go in order to be fulfilled. There is the shape of the event itself; the structure of the performance, how to begin, how to end, with decisions based both on an artistic sense of design and on the particular needs of the context and the audience. And encompassing all, the ritual and ceremony that underlie the entire performance, expressed in the quality of the performers' presence, the music, and the palpable sense of occasion—the "heightened dramatic event," as Jonathan Fox describes it.

The Role of the Conductor

The conductor embodies the fusion of art and social action: every aspect of the role carries both an aesthetic and an interactive consideration. It is the conductor who must greet and warm up the audience at the outset of the show; nothing is more crucial to the event's success. If the conductor in this initial moment is able to acknowledge and include all the disparate elements of the audience, to show a sensitivity to subgroups of age, culture, ethnicity or background, to create a sense of ease in those who are new to playback and eagerness in people who have come before, to establish an easy pattern of question and response, to direct the focus to the show's theme if there is one, then the performance is likely to unfold in a way that is satisfying to all. As the show proceeds, the conductor must remain attuned to the developing dynamics of the audience, the themes that emerge, the stories that may be untold but present. In his or her interactions with each individual teller, the conductor must create an immediate and genuine rapport, then elicit the story with grace and economy, maintaining contact with the rest of the audience while listening for the essence of the teller's experience, crystallizing it into the form of a story, and ensuring that the actors have enough but not an excess of information. As the performance draws to an end, the conductor will probably be the one to guide a closure, to draw attention to the collective story that has emerged, perhaps to thank the hosts, or to announce upcoming further events.

Are these tasks social or artistic? They are tasks that we are more familiar with in social events; but in playback they must also be fulfilled with an aesthetic attention to form, design, and style. A playback actor's adequacy is measured by his basic performance skills in combination with his attunement to the teller, the story, and his fellow-performers; a playback conductor by her assurance and skill in handling group and interpersonal connections, and by the elegance and integrity of her own demeanor.

Some conductors have, in addition to these qualities, a charm or force of personality that might be called charisma. When combined with the essential skills of the conductor, charisma can be a positive factor that draws audiences into warmth and connection. However, charisma without skill and integrity can exert power in a way that is dangerous and incompatible with "good" playback, drawing trust to a conductor who does not deserve it.

In my examples of success and failure above, fulfillment of both *artistic* and *social* considerations accounted, in my opinion, for the success of the

London and Finland performances. In London, Chloë's criticism only emphasized the fallacy of assessing a show by looking solely at what is happening on stage—in effect, by ignoring all but purely artistic criteria. In the reproductive rights performance, our artistic proficiency was not enough to make up for our shortcomings in the interactive realm.

Context and Standards

In a playback performance there is an implicit contract regarding standards between the playback team and the audience. The audience has come to see professional theatre, they have paid at the door, and they legitimately expect to see competent work. They will be disappointed and critical if the performance falls below a basic level of artistic skill. Although no audience assessment will be unanimous, there will be a general consensus about the line between adequacy and inadequacy in the use of stage, voice, movement, and the artistic shaping of scenes.

The contract is different in non-performance contexts, where stories are enacted not by a company but by members of a training or therapeutic group where there is no separately-defined audience. In a therapy group, the emphasis is entirely on the process, and there may be little if any attention paid to artistic skills. The same is true using playback with groups of managers, teachers, or social workers to help them focus on current issues in their workplace. In such settings, the participants are not expected to be skillful performers, and artistic skill on their part is not necessary to the success of the work.

However, this inherent flexibility of standards in playback does not extend to the conductor. In any context, with any group, with any purpose, the social and interactive aspects of playback must be expertly handled if the work is to fulfill itself. Whether in performances, workshops, or other applications, a sociometric awareness of the group is essential—acknowledging individuals and subgroups, inviting tellers, being alert to structures of influence and allegiance. Playback's purpose is always to bring people together, to affirm the individual and the group. Without mastery of the conductor's role, this fundamental goal cannot be achieved.

Problematic Playback Theatre

Inevitably, as playback has been adopted by enthusiasts around the world, a few have developed practices based on a fundamental misunderstanding of playback theatre's purpose. Such work can never meet the criteria for "good" playback, because it is built on distortion.

One such misapplication is the performance of playback in a comedic, entertainment manner, with little skill in sociometry or subtle communication on the part of the conductor, and insufficient respect for the story on the part of the actors. These companies may enjoy success in the sense that their audiences are enthusiastic and they may be in demand for contracted performances. However, their work is not good playback: the deeper meaning of the stories is ignored or lost, the dynamics and themes of the event remain undeveloped, and the audience is entertained without being affirmed in their humanity.

Another pitfall for playback performers, particularly conductors, is the mishandling of playback's therapeutic dimension. All playback theatre is broadly therapeutic in the sense that the process is potentially and ideally healing for all present, including the performers. Telling one's story publicly, seeing it reflected back, realizing that it is accepted and valued by others is a healing experience for the teller. For the audience, as well, there is an integration and affirmation that strengthens the connections between them. If the basic criteria for successful playback are met, this healing potential will be fulfilled. But some performers do not trust the story to carry its meaning on its own terms. Instead, with the goal of being more therapeutic, they force a "psychological" interpretation, usually with the effect of limiting instead of deepening the meaning. Actors may do this through an interpretive enactment of the scene, conductors through interpretive questions and comments during the interview. (Interpretation in the psychological sense means imposing one's therapeutic insight on the story; it is distinct from artistic interpretation, the filtering of the story through one's artistic sensibility, a process which is integral in playback.)

I once watched a conductor with a teller who told a brief but resonant story about how she survived her childhood by singing to herself whenever her family seemed too crazy. The conductor probed and delved until she elicited further information about the teller's birth and her present relationship to her family. In the enactment the teller's original story, rich with image and metaphor like a small, enigmatic painting, was buried in a rambling framework of psychological detail.

A third danger area is the failure to understand playback's vigor as theatre and its roots in oral tradition, offering it instead as a quasi-religious New Age experience replete with candles and prayers, weak in cultural reference and artistic integrity.[2]

"Good Enough" Playback Theatre

In an essay called "The Face of the Story," Mimi Katzenbach describes playback's remarkable capacity to embody meaning simply in the enactment itself. If the story is heard and enacted with empathy and an intuitive grasp of its essences, then all its multiplicity of allusion to myth, history, and psychological truth will be present and it is unnecessary, even a detraction, to make it more explicit. Playback scenes are not superficial versions of stories told to therapists. The story's meaning is in the face that it shows us; what we see there is enough.

Fortunately, the majority of playback performers are committed to its fundamental purposes. They understand the dual requirement for artistic and interpersonal sophistication; they are artists enough to respect the aesthetic qualities of story itself without distortion in the direction of psychological interpretation. And they achieve what we might call "good enough" playback, on the analogy of Bettelheim's idea of "good enough" parenting: playback that generally fulfills both the artistic and interactive criteria to an adequate degree despite inevitable shortcomings.

In striving to fulfill the work as best it can, every company faces choices about how collectively-oriented they want to be. What is more important to the group, the highest possible standards of performance or a democratic access to conducting, acting, and music? Do you leave the conducting in the hands of the most skilled, or do you commit to training everyone to conduct? Do you rotate roles during a performance as an expression of equality, in spite of a possible drop in standards? The guideline of "good enough" playback is the final determinant of how a group balances the sometimes conflicting demands of democracy and excellence.

The idea that "good enough" playback theatre depends on fulfilling the criteria for success both in art and in interactive social events has implications for training. Whether in companies or in workshops, new performers can be encouraged to develop an artist's sensibility—an aesthetic awareness of form and design, and a commitment to art's purpose of revealing meaning through inspired metaphor and image. They can also, from the beginning, learn about the need for sensitivity and skill in communication and in guiding the functioning of a group.

Many people come to playback with a background in one but not both of these areas—artists who are unsophisticated in human relationships, or helpers and healers who are undeveloped as artists. Training that emphasizes the importance of both sides can help people acquire the balance that is essential.

Trance, Subjectivity, and Judgment

The response to art and the perception of value is necessarily subjective. In playback, subjectivity of response has a special meaning, because of the marked difference in perspective between audience member, teller and performers.

For playback or any theatre to work, there must be an engagement on the part of the audience so that they allow themselves to believe in the illusion of another place and time, whether it is the Forest of Arden or the teller's childhood home. This is a kind of trance, willingly entered into by audience members. Part of the conductor's job is to entrance, to induct audience and teller into an altered state for the duration of the enactment (while remaining firmly out of trance herself). Even the actors are mildly in trance. While they remain fully aware of themselves and each other, thinking about the story and what needs to happen, they are also caught up in the reality conjured by their acting. The music is a powerful trance inducer, altering the state of the teller, audience, and actors from the first notes of the setting-up music.

The stronger the trance, the stronger the perception of success and of artistic value. The trance is almost always strongest for the teller, and weakest for the performer. All playback performers have had the experience of a teller praising them warmly after a scene that they felt they had done poorly. Audience members may also let themselves believe in a story in spite of occasional mistakes or awkwardness in the enactment. (But if the performance is not "good enough" playback, the trance will not work and audience and teller will remain unmoved.)

The peculiar strength of the teller's trance means that in non-performance situations, such as workshops, training groups, or therapy contexts, stories may be enacted with great success by people who lack skill or artistic sensibility—success in the sense that the teller and other group members feel that the story has been fulfilled satisfactorily in spite of the inexpert acting. Leading children's therapy groups, I have seen tellers completely transfixed by enactments that were clumsy and superficial, just barely adhering to the story, even though the young actors were doing as well as they could. The teller would readily project his story onto the action and feel satisfied that it had been reflected fully.

Subjectivity of response also means that the perception of artistic merit will vary according to context and expectation, as we discussed earlier. I remember a two-hour workshop for recreation workers in which a man told a story about being taken as a child to see Hooverville, the shantytown of homeless people who lived in New York's Central Park during the Depression. The man's father hoped to teach his son to appreciate the privilege and security that he had. But what Victor, the teller, remembered was the moment when a boy his own age stared back at him, a burning challenge in his eyes. In a flash Victor understood this boy's human dignity, and that it was wrong to stare as though he were an animal in a zoo. In the enactment the man who played the homeless boy fulfilled the climactic moment with unforgettable intensity and truth. He was fully invested in the role and its meaning. An experienced actor could not have done better.

He was probably to some degree in trance, believing so deeply in the reality of the boy in Hooverville that his belief informed his portrayal. Another element in the impact of his acting was the context itself, a workshop in which no-one had previous experience with playback or any other kind of performing. I and my co-leader therefore had no expectation of skillful acting and were possibly more impressed than we might have been by someone in our own company doing the same thing.

This subjectivity and flexibility of standards is not unique to playback, but in fact a component in any realm of art. Context and expectation play a part in any audience's experience of any performance. There is always an interplay between what is actually offered by the artists, on the one hand, and what the audience brings to it, on the other. The same is true of nonperformance art forms such as literature or painting. Value is ultimately a co-creation of artist and perceiver, which accounts for the genuine artistic meaning found at every point along the spectrum of actual accomplishment.

Playback's Fulfillment

In my small town there lives a world-famous pianist who performs here once or twice a year. His most recent concert fell on the same night as one of our playback shows. I was very sorry to miss it: this man's music is a treasure, a consummation of the art of the keyboard. As my imagination went from his concert, an all-Bach solo recital, to our playback theatre show, the difference between these two kinds of performances was very clear. Much as I love the magic of playback's mercurial creativity, I also sometimes want the grandeur and perfection of art that is painstakingly developed and rehearsed.

Playback is not great art. It cannot meet art's most rigorous criteria, because it is of the moment. Although performers may develop their skills for years, becoming elegant and compelling both in their acting and in the aesthetic transformation of life into theatre, their on-the-spot enactments cannot, by their nature, be built of the highly crafted language and choreography of formal theatre. However, like other art which may not attain greatness, it nevertheless has the power, depending on context and audience perception, to fulfill art's deepest purpose: the revelation of pattern and ontological meaning.

Those moments when playback reaches a peak of brilliance, those moments that we all recognize and remember, are invariably times when there has been a perfect fusion between the artistic and the interactive aspects of playback. They may happen in any setting, with inexperienced actors as well as with trained performers. In a non-performance setting, it can seem like a kind of miracle when the group members reach into themselves and discover an artist's sensibility for the first time. In my experience, this quantum leap is always called forth by a strength of emotion toward the teller and his story. It has nothing to do with a conscious striving; it is a response to humanity combined with the potency of the artist's reaching for form. The remarkable thing is that the newly-achieved level of artistry invariably creates a similar leap in the group's understanding of each other. It is a process of synergy in which the art and the group interaction mutually enhance each other.

In performance, the conductor's attunement to the audience and to the teller combines with the actors' empathy, accuracy, inspiration, and teamwork to create theatre that can be matchless in its beauty and truth.

An entire performance is unlikely to remain on such a soaring level; playback is also "Rough Theatre," in Peter Brook's phrase, with the inherent unevenness of any art whose creative process is unmasked and visible to all.

Playback theatre belongs rightfully in the realm of art; it seeks to fulfill art's fundamental purpose of revealing meaning through the aesthetic distillation of experience and perception. It is also integrally an interactive and altruistic social event. To be judged as "good," playback must fulfill the criteria for success in both these realms, as well as in those unique to playback itself.

The degree of skill required from the actors varies according to context. In performance situations, the performers must have sufficient artistry and experience to achieve "good enough" playback if they are to satisfy audience and teller. In non-performance contexts, playback can fulfill its purpose without a high degree of skill from the actors: stories may be told and enacted with satisfaction for the teller and the group as a whole in spite of a lack of experience and acting ability.

In any context, however, the conductor's artistry and interpersonal skill is necessary to playback's fulfillment. The conductor's role is an embodiment of playback's fusion of art and social action, both within and outside of performance.

And in any context, performance or otherwise, there is the possibility of those moments that show us the ideal fulfillment of playback's promise; the ephemeral, magical fusion of artistry and humanity.

References

Bateson, G. "Style, Grace, and Information in Primitive Art." In *Steps to an Ecology of Mind*. New York: Ballantine, 1972.

Bettelheim, B. *A Good Enough Parent*. New York: Vintage, 1987.

Brook, P. *The Empty Space*. New York: Avon, 1968.

Fox, J. *Acts of Service: Spontaneity, Commitment, Tradition in the Nonscripted Theatre*. New Paltz, NY: Tusitala, 1994.

Katzenbach, M. "The Face of the Story." Independent Study Essay, School of Playback Theatre, 1994.

Moreno, J. L. "Sociometry in Relation to Other Social Sciences." *Sociometry* 1 (1937): 206-219.

Newton, E. *The Meaning of Beauty*. New York: McGraw Hill, 1950.

Notes

[1] See also Salas, "Aesthetic Experience in Music Therapy," *Music Therapy*, 9, 1 (1990): 1-15.

[2] See Fox, *Acts of Service*, Part I: A Context for Nonscripted Theatre.

Playback Work with Dreams

József Parádi

"A dream is a theatre in which the dreamer is himself the scene, the player, the prompter, the producer, the author, the public, and the critic." —*C.G. Jung*

Why do I consider dreams an important topic in playback theatre?

In a significant passage on dialogue, Jung says that unless the conscious and unconscious minds learn to dialogue with equality and respect, we probably will not learn to do that person-to-person, group-to-group, or nation-to-nation.

I believe that dreams are the best means of this dialogue. Many cultures all over the world have used dreams as a basis for cultural and personal guidance. At one time, almost everyone had daily intercourse with their dream worlds. This helped to bring us culturally to where we are today. It survives mainly in folktales that must have originated "once upon a time," as somebody's dream.

I was brought up in a very materialistic family and society. We never spoke about our dreams in our family, and I learned in school that only superstitious people dealt with dreams. My university studies at medical school just made this attitude stronger. Later on as a young doctor—a neurologist—I met my patients through their laboratory findings and examination reports, and I valued scientific research based on measurements and statistics. So I was a very closed, scientific, one-sided person, and I could recall only one or two of my dreams during my first 30 years. (I couldn't sing a single song.)

My appreciation of dreams came step by step. Three things helped me to open up: my first psychological crisis, working with psychotic patients, and some altered-state-of-consciousness training.

In the first deep crisis period of my life I was shocked by countless dreams. I remembered more dreams after one night than in all my years before. But I was helpless because I couldn't do anything to understand them.

Sitting together with an acute psychotic patient on a psychiatric ward was another unusual experience for my linear thinking mind. The experience was the same as with dreams: I couldn't understand anything but I felt some deep attraction.

I began to keep a dream journal and to read books about dreams.

I was surprised how many books had been written on dreams: cognitive psychology books that viewed dreams as a complex grammar; books that provided instant symbol translations; books that critiqued all other stances, yet offered no alternative other than working with an analyst five times a week; books that interpreted, analyzed, romanticized, categorized—by culture, by function, by content, by effect, by language, by image.

This vast number of books perplexed me, but I started to use more and more methods from different books. My leading principle in this time was as follows: "If I have a methodology I do not need a dogma."

I also realized that the early pioneers in psychology did not discover the importance of dreams. They rediscovered it. It is the same story with playback theatre. Throughout the religious history of our Judeo-Christian culture, dreams played a central role in determining the fate of mankind. They were thought to be the voice of God.

With the discovery of dreams came an awakening to a new reality, a new vision of life, with dimensions I had not previously imagined.

Holotropic breath work training and some psychedelic experiences also helped me to enter into the symbolic world of the psyche. I enjoyed having dreams, keeping a dream diary, and sometimes doing something to understand and actualize my own dreams. Experiences in playback theatre gave me the last push to deal with dreams professionally.

In 1992 we formed the Improvisation Theatre of Budapest, and we began our playback work. We held two performances every month in a public theatre in Budapest.

I was very interested to see how dreams would suit the playback stage. I remember that the first dream story was a very powerful one. As an actor I was very much impressed by the dream and the enactment, and I thought we really gave something to the teller. After this experience I decided to work with dreams in and out of playback theatre.

Dream Work Activities

Nowadays I do playback work with dreams in three different contexts: in psychodrama groups; in dream workshops; in playback theatre performances.

I lead two psychodrama groups that meet for one weekend a month. From the beginning we have worked with dreams. Besides the regular psychodrama work with dreams, I developed one new method. It is a modification of Montague Ullman's four-part technique, which is a democratic and nonthreatening approach to working with dreams in a group setting. My adaptation involves playback and has four stages: in stage one the dreamer volunteers a dream, and two or three members of the group retell the dream. In stage two the group may ask questions to clarify the dream and to grasp it as clearly as possible. In stage three the group works as a playback company, and with the help of the group leader as a conductor enacts the dream on the stage. In stage four, members of the group attempt to accept the dream as it were their own, and they comment about it with the remark "If it were my dream..." This way it is clear to everyone that whatever statements follow are to be viewed as projections of the group member who is speaking. The dreamer does not respond at all during this last stage, but afterwards she is invited to respond and share how far she has come in understanding the dream.

This method needs less time than the psychodramatic enactment, and so it is useful when more than one member has a dream and wants to work with it.

In the last four years I have led two-day dream workshops. In them I teach methods from different cultures and different psychotherapeutic approaches by which the participants can enter into their dream world. In the program of the two days there is a playback performance on the first evening. For these evenings I invite our playback company, and we have a performance only with dreams. These performances are usually the high point of the two days for the participants, and our company members also especially like them.

From the beginning I felt that dreams always brought very powerful and dramatic events to the stage. Dream stories were very often turning points of the performances. These stories were crucial in the process and symbolically summarized the stories told before.

At the same time I find dreams are important indicators of company cohesion. If there is a storyteller who tells a dream, it means to me that the company is working well and the audience can trust us.

I remember a period in our history when we were busily dealing with our group process (some old members left, there were tensions between members, new conductors had begun to work, some of us still wanted to conduct, and so on). We were very tired after each performance, and we had no dream story at all for a long period.

Some members of our company shared my enthusiasm about dreams and we began to experiment. We were interested in what differences exist between everyday stories and dreams and what kind of artistic elements helped in dream enactments. We decided to have a performance with the title "Our Dreams." We had special procedures for this performance: in the rehearsal before the performance we dealt with our dreams. We began the performance with fluid sculptures, reflecting on the atmosphere of the audience members' dreams. In the middle of the performance, instead of pairs, we did the "meeting of symbols," in which three actors acted one symbol, and the other three another symbol, and they met in the middle of the stage. We finished the performance with a tableau based on the main symbols in the stories (I presented the result of our experiments at the Sixth International Playback Theatre Conference in Perth, Australia in 1997).

I think two factors are important in working with dreams in playback theatre—safety and discovery. The safety factor is necessary because the dreamer is exposing a most personal and vulnerable side of himself. He needs to feel assured that he will be heard, the control will remain in his hands, and in a way that respects his privacy and authority over the dream. The discovery factor comes into play when we have to respond to another need of the dream teller—namely, to be helped to make discoveries about himself that are difficult to make alone.

The conductor has an important role in providing these elements and in finding the right balance. In the case of dreams there is a temptation to place the teller in the center, and to do some kind of "clinical playback." I think that in a theatre context we have to resist this temptation. It is better not to be concerned with deeper layers of meaning and to avoid any kind of "interpretative enactment." Instead we can choose a phenomenological approach to dreams, emphasizing a detailed questioning in the interview and the artistic richness of the enactment.

Transformations in Dream Work

The reason why we almost never transform a dream is that it is so important for tellers to see their images as they dreamt them. This is counter to psychodramatic practice, which seems always to extend and transform. In theatre it is better when we can be detailed and rich but enigmatic in the enactment and leave the extension and the transformation to the fantasy of the teller and audience.

The only exception is the persecution dream, in which somebody or something is pursuing the dreamer. In this case in the transformation we let the dreamer and the persecutor meet and have a dialogue.

In the King Arthur legend there was an old king who was very ill and could only be healed when a knight asked the right question. We might look at that mythic story as a metaphor for working with dreams in playback theatre. This is a great challenge for the conductor.

Dream logic is antithetical to waking logic. It is an acausal logic that exists in a timeless, spatially unbound universe. Unconsciously influenced by Western "beginning-middle-end", and "cause-and-effect" story structure we make our dreams conform to our storytelling habits. Many dreams are stories indeed. Yet many dreams are not stories at all but a series of images, natural plays, paintings, poems. These dreams are real challenges for playback theatre. Organic images are destroyed if we subject them to linear thinking. How often do we judge them as "bizarre" or "weird"? They need to be allowed to grow like plants in a spiraling movement. They carry emotional and imaginative energy as well as intellectual meaning.

I remember once our company performed a dream fragment about a beautiful branch on a cherry tree. The actors connected physically to each other and sang a wonderful Hungarian song about the rebirth of nature and the world, and the audience was deeply pleased.

The enactment of dreams gives us an excellent possibility for breaking the usual linear, causal logic. That's why we usually start the enactment of a dream with a stage picture. We use lot of colorful cloth, intensive music and lights. We often use mime and gibberish. We often use dreams in our rehearsals when we want to practice non-linear enactments. We did a lot of experimenting with changing the rhythm of our movements. Slowing down every movement during the enactment became a favorite technique in the enactment of dreams.

Once in a rehearsal our company enacted a dream of mine in slow motion. I felt that the slow motion transformed my dream into a meditation object, and I could sit and just contemplate it. We do not always need to fully "understand" dreams to receive their gifts. Rather, we can circumambulate them, respect them, let their images feed our imagination and lead us onward.

In summary, these are my suggestions concerning playback and dreams. It is a good sign when someone wants to tell a dream in a public performance, for it means the audience can trust the company. Fragments and image enactment are acceptable when acting dreams. Instead of interpreting, extending, or transforming a dream, we have detailed questioning in the interview and a rich but enigmatic enactment (theatre versus psychotherapy). In the enactment of a dream we use colorful cloth, intensive music and lights, miming, gibberish and a conscious change in the actors' rhythm. Finally, since dreams are useful for breaking linear, causal logic, they are very helpful for acting practice in rehearsals.

References

Boa, Fraser. *The Way of the Dream: Conversation on Jungian Dream Interpretation with Marie-Luise von France.* London: Shambhala, 1994.

Fox, Jonathan. *Acts of Service: Spontaneity, Commitment, Tradition in the Nonscripted Theatre.* New Paltz, NY: Tusitala Publishing, 1994.

Jung, C.G. *Memories, Dreams, Reflections.* New York: Vintage Books, 1965.

_____. *Dreams.* London: Ark, 1991.

Mellick, Jill. *The Natural Artistry of Dreams: Creative Ways to Bring the Wisdom of Dreams to Waking Life.* Berkeley: Conari Press, 1996.

Petrovits, Jovan. *Ten Haikus to R.I.A. for the Birth of Spirituality.* Arizona Press, 1964.

Salas, Jo: *Improvising Real Life: Personal Story in Playback Theatre.* New Paltz, NY: Tusitala Publishing, 1993.

Sullwold, Edith. "Dream as a Story." In *Sacred Stories.* C. & A. Simpkinson, ed. San Francisco: Harper, 1993.

Ullman, M. & N. Zimmerman. *Working with Dreams.* Los Angeles: Jeremy Tarcher, 1985.

Van de Castle, R. L. *Our Dreaming Mind: The Role of Dreams in Politics, Art, Religion and Psychology from Ancient Civilizations to the Present Day.* London: Aquarian, 1994.

Williams, S. K. *The Dreamwork Manual: A Step-by-Step Introduction to Working with Dreams.* London: Aquarian Press, 1984.

Playback Portrait

ORLA MCKEAGNEY
Northern Ireland

Orla McKeagney, aged 27, is a woman from a war-torn land. From a Catholic family, she first learned of the possibility of community reconciliation when two Protestant girls taught her a song at the back of a school bus. She was only a primary school kid then, but has never forgotten that song.

Orla worked for a theatre company after finishing university, but now is an independent "drama facilitator." In a typical week, she leads a variety of workshops and classes—with 14-16 year-olds, with university theatre degree students, with youth workers, with stroke patients. To help make ends meet, she sings in a jazz group and works in a clothes shop.

Orla first heard of playback theatre in a university course focussing on community drama, but she says she didn't really take notice of playback theatre until she came across Jo Salas's book in a shop. "That's when it started," she says. Since that time, she has traveled twice to the USA, last year graduating from the School of PT in New York.

Playback theatre is "one of the more challenging techniques to use," Orla says. "It doesn't work if you've only got 20 minutes for it." What is a good minimum exposure? "Four hours," she says.

In 1996, Orla founded a PT company consisting of Catholic and Protestant actors. For a variety of reasons, including the strain of the Northern Irish context, the group eventually disbanded, but not before they did important work together. Orla wrote about one moment:*

Rather surprisingly, James, aged 27, a worker in the retail sector

---

* See "The Contribution PT Can Make to the Northern Ireland Situation," Independent Study Essay, School of Playback Theatre, 1998.

who initially had been one of the more resistant members of the group to the opening up process, became the instigator of a marked change in relationships between the members. He had related his feelings at his grandfather's funeral when he was six years of age and recalled the pain and bitterness expressed by his parents and other relatives at his grandfather's killing by the IRA. His father had told him never to trust Catholics as all of them were as suspect as those who had murdered his grandfather. It was the first time in his life to relate the incident publicly. The re-creation in drama proved to be a very powerful experience for all of us and was instrumental in breaking down the reluctance to confronting the core issues of the Northern Ireland conflict that had been prevalent for so long.

Mary, a Catholic teacher, had been picked to play the role of James' father. Afterwards she expressed her feeling of guilt that a fellow Catholic could have carried out such an act, and expressed her revulsion at the extremes to which some were prepared to go in order to create an alternative political system. She also observed that the experience had enabled her to acquire an understanding about how prejudice in her own family had been passed down the generations. As a consequence, she felt that her own natural instincts about the current situation might merit re-examination. Michael, the other teacher who had voiced support for the on-going guerrilla action to change the existing political structure, felt the need, likewise, to question some of his own attitudes, given the pain one past incident, to which he had never considered expressing opposition previously, had inflicted on James and others who came from a section of the population holding similar views.

Orla is eagerly awaiting her upcoming chance to introduce play-back theatre to members of Columbanus, an organization devoted to peace and reconciliation in Northern Ireland. "I know they will understand what PT can do," she says. But such opportunities have been few and far between. "We are not so open as a community," she says, making silent reference to the decades of conflict in her homeland. "It's so painful."

She doesn't know when she will be ready to encourage both Catholic and Protestant groups to tell their stories in front of each other. She talks about a feeling of loneliness in her role as a PT conductor/facilitator.

Bringing playback theatre to a new region is always a formidable challenge, but in Northern Ireland it can feel overwhelming: "I often wonder why I am doing this. But I can't let go of it. PT is always there. There's something so right about it. It feels right to do." Almost in the same breath, Orla shares her dream: "I want to establish a PT performance group in Belfast, one that would be funded and validated both for theatre and as a community organization."

The Red Thread

Storytelling as a Healing Process

Folma Hoesch [1]

Playback theatre has a deep effect on people who tell their stories and on groups in which stories are told and played back. Although it is not psychotherapy, I would like to say that it is healing.[2]

Playback theatre is a new approach to theatre, built on the tradition of oral culture. There is no written text, nobody knows beforehand what is going to be told and enacted.

Playback theatre has a certain form. It is a vessel in which something can come into existence. Although the content is unknown beforehand, a sense of order rather than chaos prevails. Each time something unique evolves, there is a process. One can see the meaning of it clearly, at least by looking back on it. In a short time, a group is created whether people knew each other before or not—a group with its own theme, with a red thread.[3] There is a clear path rather than a labyrinth; there is a definite way in, a center and a way out.

At the beginning of a playback event we face the unknown. We feel both openness and anxiety. We trust that once again something will come into being that has a gestalt and a meaning, through which community will be created.

Usually the people who discuss and write about playback theatre actually do it, as actors, conductors, musicians. In this essay my perspective is that of the spectators and the tellers of stories.

From this point of view a series of questions arise: why does a person tell a story? How does someone come to be a teller? To whom am I telling my story? Am I telling it to the conductor, who invited me and others to tell? Am I talking to the other spectators or seminar participants? Do I want to hear myself telling? Do I want to see what I tell? Which story am I going to present? And how much is this related to my personal history, how much does it have to do with the group in which the story is told? When in the group's process do which stories get told? These are many questions. I cannot answer them all, but I feel challenged to ask them and think about them and express my thoughts in writing. I am interested especially in one aspect: how is a story connected with the stories that were told beforehand?

During playback performances or among groups who do playback we find again and again that the stories respond to each other and furthermore, that they offer patterns for solution and transformation. To me this means that something is happening that is doing good and can be healing both for the individual member and for the group as a whole.

To get to know more about this phenomenon I chose a very pragmatic approach: I will retell stories that were told in a two-week seminar which I attended, and think about the connections between them. My main interest will be in the motifs of the stories. Which elements, motifs, figures from a story come up in a later one? How do they connect? From these observations, I will build a hypothesis about how stories come into being, how they are generated from each other, and further, how we can look at the life of a group and understand the relation between the individual and the whole.

Two Women Tell a Story

On the morning of her 55th birthday, Anna was sitting in a seminar with Jonathan Fox near Bern in Switzerland. She had decided not to tell anybody about her birthday because she still felt a little unconnected to this group. Erna, a young person sitting next to her, seemed to be in a depressed mood. When Anna asked her how she was doing she said that her father had died the day before. She had found out only early that morning, since her contact with her family was not very good. She did not want to go see her mother now, but rather to take part in the seminar as circumspectly as possible, without saying anything about it. This coincidence of birth(day) and death touched both women deeply. In the following go-round, Erna decided to speak about the death of her father, and Anna mentioned her birthday. Both got a lot of sympathy, congratulations, and little signs of thoughtfulness during the day.

In the evening of this day Jonathan offered Erna the chance to have the group play something back for her. She told the following story: *Yesterday I brought my sandwich for lunch as usual because I did not want to go with the others to the restaurant, which was loud and expensive. So I walked by myself on a sunny path, which led me unexpectedly to a cemetery. After having lunch there I walked between the graves and read the inscriptions on the tombstones. I was amazed how many times they said something about thankful children and loving parents. Late that night I came home. My answering machine was blinking, one of my sisters wanted to talk to me urgently. Although it was very late, I called, but when she didn't pick up the phone right away I gave up. The next morning I called my sister again, but her phone was busy. So I called my mother. She was crying, unable to talk. Now I knew what had happened: my father had died. But I didn't want to go home and I decided to come to the seminar even if this was very egoistic.*

The three scenes were played back to Erna. After this Jonathan asked her whether she wanted to see something else. And now she wondered about how her father died because she did not know. And she generated a fantasy about her father's last moments: She assumed that amidst the turmoil of her mother's loud emotional outbursts, her father had died alone and unobserved, almost happy to leave all the trouble behind.

This scene was also enacted. Erna was thankful and sat down again. The group and especially Anna were deeply touched by Erna's story and her father's lonely death. Still immersed in these images and feelings, Anna was very surprised when Jonathan invited her to tell a story, too, as a birthday present and as closure for the day. Without any idea what to tell she sat in the teller's chair. In order to help her, Jonathan asked about her at progressively younger ages, to help her find a story. In Anna's head was the notion of birthdays, and she thought about the different birthday parties that her mother had created for her during her childhood. She recalled photographs of these parties, which she kept in an album. But all this somehow didn't feel important enough, it seemed empty and didn't touch her. She even felt a slight aversion to bringing her mother into the picture. All of a sudden it became clear what she wanted to tell. A feeling of warmth went through her whole body, the stream of images stopped, and she felt an opening in her heart.

Anna recounted: *For the past few years I've kept a photo by my bedside of me at six months old with my father. It is the only existing photo of my father and me, because a few weeks later he was called in as a soldier, was later taken as prisoner of war, and went missing in Russia. I would like to see the scene when the photo was taken: my father is sitting on the grass in our garden with his baby on his lap. Both are smiling. A few meters in front of them my mother is kneeling down with the camera. We are a happy family, at least in this moment. Far away, in the background, the war is already present.*

Until this evening Anna had never realized that the photo of her and her father must have been taken by her mother, that her mother is present though invisible. For Anna, the enactment of her story was the most beautiful birthday present she could think of.

Looking at the two stories I realized only later that there is a close connection between Anna's story and Erna's story. Erna's story is about being alone and being together, belonging and not belonging, pulling back because there is no peaceful security in her family. She talks about it in several variations: her lunch by herself, apart from the group, the difficulties in getting in touch with her sister, the impossibility of talking to her mother, the fantasy about her father's lonely death in the midst of the family. At the edge of the story, the motif of love between parents and children appears in the tombstone inscriptions—which are surprising and even strange to Erna.

In Anna's life, love between parents and child and an intact family could not exist because the war destroyed everything. In her experience of family there was no father, so she wouldn't consciously have sought out a father-daughter scene. Nevertheless, the photo came to her mind, and she chose precisely the only scene in which father, mother and daughter were present and deeply connected.

I have told this story, of which I know the interior perspective and the preceding history, in order to use it as an example. This background knowledge is rare in playback theatre, because the stories are not commented on, analyzed, or worked out therapeutically.

In summary of this sequence I want to underline the following aspects. The second story responds to the first. Nobody is consciously looking for such a connection; the tellers themselves are totally unaware of it. Some motifs appear on several levels. The feeling of not belonging comes up already at the beginning of the day, when both women plan not to say anything about the special experiences they are going through. It leads like a red thread through Erna's story and finds a counterpoint in the story of Anna. This element, the feeling of belonging together, already arose in the tombstone inscriptions, holding surprise and a slight shock for the teller.

There is a level of feeling, thinking and telling with which the tellers identify. They think, "I had better not say anything because I don't really belong to these people around me." And there is another level with which they both do not identify—safety, love and togetherness.

Here I am drawing on Arnold Mindell's model of process-oriented psychology to describe these two sides of the storytelling process.[4] Mindell describes stream of consciousness as a process of signals being sent and perceived. Instead of dividing the soul into the conscious and the unconscious as other approaches do, he distinguishes between the part with which a person is identifying, i.e. what he accepts as all right for himself and others, and the other side with which he does not identify—i.e., what he does not accept, what he sees as outside of himself, what he thinks he cannot do or must not do, what is disturbing for him or what he is even fighting against in himself or in others. "People identify with their intentions or 'primary' process. 'Secondary' processes are experienced as being foreign and distant."[5] The secondary happens unwillingly to them. Mindell uses the terms primary and secondary very differently from what we are used to in other sciences.

Between both sides of the process there is an edge.[6] A person says for example: "I cannot do this." Probably she does not want to get into a discussion or a fight with somebody, or she feels unable to do it. However, this matter is troublesome for her; again and again it shows up in her life; it is somehow knocking at her door. The edge holds a lot of energy. There are strong prohibitions around it, bad experiences, negative images. To step over the edge consciously is not easy. The signals from the edge are strong hints about a person's frontier of growth.

I use this psychological model for the process of telling stories as well. The different motifs are looked at like the different parts or figures within the individual or the different members or roles in groups. The edge appears in the feelings and values of the tellers. In our stories we find Erna having trouble believing that the inscriptions on the tombstones are to be taken seriously, and Anna not even thinking of the possibility that her family had been complete at the beginning. Erna expresses the edge clearly, by showing her estranged feelings about the inscriptions. She cannot totally trust these expressions of love because her experiences in this field were negative. The secondary motif is connected with other people. Looking at Anna we see the edge in the fact that it never came into her awareness that the photo was taken by her mother. The experience of a whole family is secondary for her. Being invited to tell a story without having a plan, an aspect could come up which was new and surprising for her.

The edge can also arise in a more blatant way, such as somebody saying, "I cannot do this or that," or "I don't like this, I hate this..." We will see this in the stories I will discuss later. Primary for both tellers is the feeling of not belonging to the group, either the family or the seminar. Secondary—i.e., outside their definition of themselves in this moment, is community, togetherness, and love. The secondary motifs seem to wait until they can show up in a different way. In them we find the power of change.

The terms conscious and unconscious don't seem to fit here because the whole process is happening more or less consciously. The tellers actively decide how to shape their stories. But it seems to me that there are forces of the soul working which are not planned and cannot be planned. In playback theatre we use the word spontaneity for this.[7] And in the end this is what I am discussing. But how it happens in detail, how the forces interact, how they complete each other and make a whole with the potential of healing: that is my question, and I want to collect more examples to explore it.

Connecting Stories

In the beginning of a playback event there is quite often a feeling of discomfort. Nobody knows what is about to happen, neither actors nor visitors. The stomach is a little uneasy, feels empty, the brain seems to be somewhat dizzy. We sit on a spectator's seat and ask ourselves: "Do I want to get involved here? Do I feel like telling a story? And if I wanted to, will a story come to my mind? Do I have anything to talk about? Or is my life totally uninteresting for others? I could easily feel embarrassed if I say anything." Nobody seems to know the rules here.

A group, like an individual, has a primary process, issues and ideologies with which they identify, and a secondary process, consisting of the things that happen to them with which they do not want to identify. Most primary processes are connected with issues. The secondary ones are usually emotional and are concerned with hurt, happiness, power struggles and spiritual needs, all of which the group has an edge against. "The primary process is the sense of 'we' which the members refer to, the thing which makes the family or group different from others... A city's local environment or a nation's myth may be primary." [8]

The primary process of a playback group is very open. There is a connecting idea, especially if it is not our first playback evening. It could be something like, Stories will be told and acted out here, and it is new and fascinating. But this idea works more like a "blank access," an open approach with low structure, without content, and with only a few rules of behavior for the visitors. [9]

On the other hand, the tellers do choose what to tell and there are connections between stories that are conscious, or at least very close to how a person is identifying at the given moment. That is what I want to talk about now, before I get to the secondary elements.

Like many other seminars and evenings, our week in Bern began with stories about leaving home, travelling, arrival, etc. The actual situation of the participants is the connecting element. Somebody plucks up courage and tells something. But to whom? To the conductor? Of course, he invited them and that is important. They feel welcomed. Or is it to the other group members? Maybe I am curious and a little restless; I like to show myself, to be seen, to take space. Or do I tell the story to myself? Do I need to make myself feel that I am here, not just present, watching, participating, but actively here in this place in this moment? The teller takes a role in an open field. The role can be: I am active, I am not a quiet one without courage. It can also be: I am helpful, I'm helping this event get started. Or it can come from other motivations. The group begins to generate a structure. A community creates itself by taking roles.

Like the different roles, the stories being told in this beginning phase don't look alike. A few examples:

Fritz comes up as the first teller in our seminar. *I was early at the station this morning. Usually I am late and in a hurry. But today I had time to go to a bookshop and buy a postcard. It shows a man flying over the city, while standing on a book. With pleasure I watched people running around. A little later I got on the bus where a friendly Spanish woman explained to me where to get off.*

After this we hear and see the story about Erica's chaos: *I was in the middle of moving. I was staying at my friend's place. Her husband was opposed to my being there because nobody had told him beforehand. There was a lot to organize with boxes and things, and I didn't know how to cope anymore. My husband had already left totally exhausted for the new city and was not available to help. But then my friend's husband became very caring and helpful. Unfortunately, I missed my chance to say goodbye to him, because everything was so rushed and chaotic.*

The two stories stand in deliberate contrast to each other. Surprisingly they show the tellers from a very unusual side, a side even somewhat unknown to the tellers themselves. Normally things are more the other way around. Fritz is always in a hurry. Erica is well organized and does not live in chaos. And the opposite motif comes up in both stories: in Fritz's scene there are other people at the station running around, and in Erica's story the caring friends maintain overview and organization. The mentally conscious identity and the secondary parts seem to be mixed. Their roles seem to be exchanged. Is there a special reason for this? Do we pay attention to what is unusual about ourselves because it is different from everyday life? I would like to leave this question for later.

I especially want to highlight the friendly Spanish woman helping Fritz in the bus. The question of who is Swiss and who is a foreigner, or who feels at home and who is far away from his origins, is another variation of the theme of belonging and feeling estranged and will be a very important theme in this seminar.

In the process of beginning, roles are created for the different members of the group, as well as a beginning structure and a first feeling of "we are a group." A special state of consciousness is evolving. As people from a Western culture we are used to thinking, analyzing, explaining, and understanding what happens. These explanations are not necessarily expressed. They are clear for everybody. But we love to give speeches, write essays, make up paradigms to explain things. Playback theatre does not explain. The stories will not be commented on. After a scene is acted out the conductor will ask the teller whether what the actors played is like what she told. Only if she feels that something really was different, does not fit or was even hurtful, will she say: "No, it was different." In this case, the conductor can decide to let the actors play it again. Or, and this can be just as appropriate, the initial enactment is accepted as a variation of what happened. Quite often the actors have picked up on a secondary element, which the teller had not seen so far or did not have access to. But most of the time the tellers say: "Yes, this is how it was." We all know that it cannot have been like this. The story in itself has fictional aspects and the play even more. The players do not use costumes or make-up. A few boxes and colored pieces of fabric define the stage, words are improvised and music underlines the scene. This is not what the teller experienced in the first place. Something like a miracle is happening here.

It seems to me that two very simple facts are important: It is very unusual for us to tell our own stories to an audience and it is even more unusual that we can watch them. We hardly ever see our own life from outside, we do not look at it on a stage, we do not think of it as fiction. Playback theatre does not comment or judge, there is no explanation or understanding with words and terms. We just watch. That puts us in a different state of consciousness very quickly. A slight trance is created. We begin to "think" in stories and pictures, we watch and add stories to other stories, fit pictures to pictures without our rational primary process getting started. In his book *Acts of Service*, Jonathan Fox shows us that trance induction is part of preliterary acting.[10] It is surprising to me how quickly a slight trance is created only by the means of telling and watching.

A moment of irritation, disorientation, slight chaos is a necessary element of this process. Only when I give up wanting to understand what I experience in rational terms will this trance work for me and evolve as a source of creativity.

The Connections Between Several Stories
At the beginning of the process, tellers often reveal stories that show themselves in a positive light. Here I want to talk about a very different aspect,

that part of the evening or seminar when stories are told which are especially difficult for the protagonists, where somebody broke down or failed or didn't act at all like a hero. One can imagine that a certain trust is necessary. People need to feel safe and it is important that they have had the opportunity before to show that they were not always in a bad position or in the role of the victim. Sometimes the way in can come from a conscious articulation of one of the red threads already part of the group theme.

During the second week of our seminar, there was an afternoon when the tellers, adult men and women, many of them teachers, talked about childhood experiences where they felt abandoned.

Fritz started: *I am 12 years old, home alone; my mother is at work and pays little attention to me. I go to visit her in the shoe shop where she sells shoes, to be closer to her. But I feel that I am tiresome, she doesn't have time for me. In the evening she comes home. She talks about what happened during the day, but she tells only my father, not me. I feel excluded and alone.*

The next one to talk was Richard: *In my story I am 12 years, too. I am on my way home from school. The other kids tease me, they bully and bother me. I am afraid and sick of it at the same time, I want to be left alone. I take my book bag and swing it around me on one of its straps. They have to give up and leave me in peace. In school I was a lot better than they were, especially in French. My book bag was my weapon.*

Both tellers are the same age in their stories; both are alone. But their experience is totally different. Fritz does not get enough attention, he feels put off, and he misses love. Yet he cannot do anything about it. Richard gets too much attention, but he is able to fight.

This motif becomes the trigger for a third story. Ingrid says: *I was 13. It was just before we were given our report cards in school. The teacher told me to come up to him after class. As soon as I could I ran up to him in the hallway. He turned to me and told me in front of all the other students that my grades were very bad. I felt very embarrassed because everybody was watching.*

After the scene had been enacted, the conductor, this time a member of the group, offered Ingrid a transformation of her story. This time she creates a scene in which the teacher talks to her in a place where she feels protected, and he is more understanding. The group members who played teasing pupils before are now in the role of the protecting wall around the encounter.

The main motifs in this story are the same: age, feeling left alone, feeling put down. The missing part of the first story, the protective loving atmosphere, is replaced in the second story by the fight, the self-protection, and pushing away the schoolmates. In the transformation of the third story it is possible to find a situation and a figure incorporating protection and love: the understanding teacher.

These connections are easy to recognize. This phase of the group process is characterized by a good feeling of trust. On the other hand, we have to consider that group members are now conducting. They are taking risks; the task is new and exciting for them. That may well be a reason why there are stories about schooldays and feelings of fear and loneliness. The tellers know what they are going to tell before they come up to the stage. They have primary reasons and we can expect that primary motifs are the connecting elements between the stories.

The second story seems to give the teller of the first story a clue that he could have helped himself and fought for his needs. But I am quite sure that Richard did not do this on purpose. It seems to me that the second teller offers an alternative, a solution in which the active and passive roles are exchanged. Fritz is a victim of desolation, Richard wants to be left alone. The third story ends with a transformation. It brings a kind of peace. The stories do not finish in an open-ended or unsettled fashion, and the process of telling comes into balance. The atmosphere in the group is relaxed now. The next story can address another theme.

In this story, the central motif is carried on. A person is alone and needs care because of this. Urs talks about his old mother: *She is living in her own apartment, and I worry about her. I need to check on her, but she doesn't pick up the telephone. My fourteen year-old son has the clue: this is the time when grandmother takes a bath, and so she cannot answer the phone. But the whole family is fed up because there is so much trouble.* The motif of being alone and needing help is seen from a very different perspective here. For the teller it is not in the realm of his normal routine, and it eats at him.

The motifs make a chain, but they are not put together like pearls. They connect in a very special way. In the first story the main motif is brought up, but there is no solution. In a secondary way—i.e., in connection with other people, the solution is present: Fritz's parents are connected—they talk to each other and listen. But this doesn't help the protagonist. He feels excluded.

The next story shows a very different solution, and it shifts the perspective. The teller is not the victim anymore, but he is an active hero, who fights for his goals. But he stays alone at the end. In this nothing has changed. In the third story the motif is different yet again. The teller feels alone and unprotected as in the first story. She, too, does not come up with a solution right away. But in the transformation she can point the way to finding protection and support.

Missing elements of one story are told in the next one. But the whole solution is not found in one step, but rather is built up in several steps. The fourth story brings in a new perspective and places a different role at the center. It is the son who can express that he feels oppressed by his mother's needs and his ex-wife's pressure. I think it is remarkable that the motif of age, which connected the first three stories, appears again at the edge. The teller's son who knows that grandmother is taking her bath at this time of day is the same age as Fritz, Richard, and Ingrid in their stories.

Finding the Theme

There was a unique composition of people in our seminar. The vast majority were teachers, mainly from primary schools but also high school, college and university level. A minority were psychologists. Some people were trained as both teachers and psychologists. Men and women were there in more or less equal numbers. Ages were balanced pretty much between thirties and mid-fifties. The most striking characteristic was the distribution of nationalities. The majority of members were Swiss. Only two members were foreigners, a Greek woman and a German one. The only full-time psychologist was a man formerly from the Alsace, a part of France belonging to Germany and France at different historical times and occupied by the Nazis in World War II. Everybody had been living in Switzerland for a long time. In this area one could find a clear majority and minority as well. In addition, the leader of the seminar, Jonathan Fox, was American. This very fact gave a special importance to the minority of "foreigners." The relatively strong borders of the Swiss group were opened up in an important aspect.

I mention this constellation in detail because it was very significant in the process of finding the group's theme during this two-week seminar.

My being German made me a member of a minority that faces quite a few prejudices in Switzerland because of history. This certainly influenced my awareness. I think it was sharpened.

I had already had a long talk with André, the man from Alsace, during our first lunch. He is my age, which means we both experienced World War II as the overwhelming element of our childhood, but from very different perspectives. Our encounter was very open-minded and brought us in good contact instead of separating us, as it could have. At the time, in 1995, the theme of World War II was relatively far away for Swiss people. (This has changed a lot in the meantime.) None of the other people present in the group had experienced it. It had not played an important role in the history of their families. World War II used to be a part of the national myth—the myth of the heroic soldier defending the Swiss border against the evil surrounding the country.

On the second day of the seminar André came forward as a teller after Jonathan had asked me to be the conductor. André told: *When I was three years old my father had to hide from the Nazis. My mother used to bring him food and provide him with information every night. So my 13 year-old brother and I were alone at home very often. One night my brother was so terribly afraid that he trembled with his whole body, and I walked him around our apartment in order to help him relax. This memory came back to my mind this morning when I had to leave my 15 year-old son alone at home because he needs to stay in bed with a fever. I could hardly do it. But I promised to talk to our neighbor and to his older sister and to call him to find out how he is doing.*

The two scenes were played, the second as a transformation of the first. I must say I was touched very deeply by the fact that André told this story in this setting with me, a German woman, as the conductor, and I mentioned this to him. In response André gave me a chestnut he had picked up in front of the building, saying that chestnuts surely must have been one of the main childhood toys for me, too. The experience of war gave us a strong connection in front of the Swiss group members, who, as we assumed in that moment, had played with "real" toys, not chestnuts. A minority is uniting here, bringing up a theme they usually have to hold back, because it does not have a great resonance in everyday Swiss life. What is not part of the identity of the majority comes up as a theme of the minority. The secondary is made "primary."

I make the hypothesis that the later stories about loneliness, fear, feeling excluded and excluding oneself, i.e. wanting to be independent, are variations of this motif which was raised in the very beginning. In connection with majority and minority, the historical and political elements come into play—in Jung's terms, the collective aspect.[11]

And now, to underline my hypothesis, a second story: The seminar included a whole lot of experiments of how to use playback in school. In this phase Eugen, who works in the field of ongoing teacher training, projected a photo on a screen both as a trigger of stories and as a background for the stage. It showed an old Mediterranean house with flowerpots in the windows. In the middle, a door, on either side two old people on chairs, and in front a big dog. Eugen asked the group to "find" stories to go with this picture.

Jakob recounts the following: *Several years after the war the old parents sit in front of their house in the sun. They have waited for many years for their son to come back from being prisoner of war. But so much time has passed, and they are about to give up hope. From far away a tired young man approaches. He is walking very slowly, because he is sick and weak. The two old people don't notice him. But the dog jumps up and runs toward the man, wagging his tail. Everybody is very happy about the return.*

By telling this story a fundamental rule of playback theatre was broken. The conductor did not ask for a self-experienced story. When Jakob is questioned, he remembers that his grandmother told him this story, her own experience, when he was an adolescent. And it touched him a lot. The group, too, was deeply touched by the story and the enactment as well. We needed a long feedback round to contain all the feelings. We can see here that a collective theme was brought up—the return of the prodigal son, and with it the return to feeling at home, belonging to the community, the broken wholeness, and the healing of it.

By the way, the photo was an advertisement for an absolutely banal product. Some of the group members knew it from television. Jakob did not. We had a discussion at this point about why it is so important to tell stories from one's own experience in playback settings. The spreading out of the feelings into the group is unavoidable if stories have a collective aspect and are not connected with a personal history. This can break the frame in which playback is working.

On the other hand, we can see the power playback theatre contains. Our seminar took place in 1995. The Swiss identity of being a neutral country which had not participated in World War II was intact. Half a year later the complaints about Swiss banks holding back information about Jewish bank accounts started a new process of reflecting on Switzerland's role during the Nazi era. Today, in 1998, the public discussion is still going on and step by step the country is finding a new primary identity. Looking back on our seminar I think that the theme was already in the field, and a mixed group like ours was picking it up and working on it.

A Contribution to Understanding Groups

I want to use this story to address the question of how groups work and become creative, or to be more exact, to explore which paradigm about groups can help us understand the relationship between the individual and the group.

As a first step I go back to that single spectator, the teller of a story. Playback theatre works with scenes, series of scenes, living pictures. Nothing is commented on or analyzed. The images remain. For most of us living in Western countries, this works as a trance induction, as mentioned above.

We can best compare this state of mind to a dream. In dreams, too, nothing is explained, commented on or analyzed, the pictures speak for themselves. And they have their own logic. Jung called the logic of dreams compensatory.[12] The dream shows me something about myself which I don't see. It is closely connected with the present situation in my life, but the central point is outside my own awareness. It shows me my own experience from a totally different viewpoint and makes more visible what I am not observing clearly. Often the dream leads to a solution in difficult situations, which would not otherwise come to mind. It seems to me that the altered state of consciousness of the spectators in playback theatre opens this kind of dreamlike logic, and that the connections between stories can be understood according to the way we look at dreams.

In this dreamlike state the secondary elements of personal processes become more accessible. The edge, holding us back from the secondary stuff in our everyday controlled state of being awake, has much less energy and can be overcome as easily as in dreams. This happens particularly if somebody is invited to tell unexpectedly and has no time to think about it, plan or become fearful. This is why the stories of Erna and Anna demonstrate especially clearly how the surprising parts, the strange elements come into play, and how the healing power of life starts working.

In psychodrama we describe the soul as some kind of stage where inner figures play a huge drama.[13] They fight against each other, they help each other, they block and complement each other perfectly. In the best case they build a beautiful whole in which many different creative powers work together and create a rich life. But the intrapsychic figures have a grave difficulty: they all have more or less the same history. They had the same parents, fought against the same outer conditions, and they usually have the same blocks and edges. The roles are pretty fixed through the life they all have in common. Changes are always changes of the whole system bringing everything out of balance, and that is why they release a lot of fear for other inner and of course outer figures.

When we think about a group in this way, it is basically the same. The individual group members correspond to the inner figures. They act together. The loud ones overwhelm the silent, some have a central role, others stay on the margin. There are majorities dominating the process and minorities being overpowered or silenced and sometimes disruptive.

In recent years, groups are often looked at under the model of the field, and different elements from field theory are applied in the description of groups.[14] Groups have certain roles. One member or a small subgroup takes the leadership role, sometimes explicitly, more often from the background. Others are the opponents, the critics. Some do not say much, but they feel a lot and are often very sensitive. Each group has its own majority. It is defined according to the goals of the group and the ideas the group is following. The more clearly the goal is defined, the more clearly the majority can be defined. From this, a minority always emerges. But it does not always become evident in the same way. The goal of the majority corresponds to the primary process of the group, the minority represents the secondary process.

It is not clear at the beginning who is going to be the minority. If, for example, everybody is tired, the eager ones who want to go on are the minority. If most of the people in the group are Swiss and two non-Swiss members feel connected by the theme of the war it can easily happen that their experiences during World War II become a secondary theme. This can be on two different levels at the same time: for the minority it is a real experience and for the majority it is unknown and it becomes an archetype, a basic pattern of fear. The minority is channeling an important theme of the majority, which is repressed in everyday life.

Between the two parts there is an edge. As long as the majority insists on its primary goal and wants to keep its balance (homeostasis), the secondary part is looked at as irritation, disturbance, even as a hostile element. The more the goal is emotion-laden, the more a group will become polarized.

Mindell works with the concept that each group is able to find new solutions if it is possible to give each of the parts enough space to express themselves and maintain fairness for all sides. "Filling the role of the leader, the follower, the silent one, the wise one or the disturber is essential for the life of the community. Only when all the roles are filled and interact, can the entire field discover its own human and self-governing capacity." [15] Groups naturally own the power to find a way to balance and harmony and experience themselves anew as whole. "If there is a tendency to create and express itself, it dreams itself to conclusion ... creating a new and unpredictable collective center, a numinous community experience." [16]

In playback theatre groups don't have a theme at the beginning. People want to be together, experience something new; they hope to find nice entertainment and to feel good. This is a very open attitude. Nevertheless a structure is created and a sequence of stories with a red thread appears in a short period.

One aspect seems especially important to me. The people getting together for a playback performance usually have only loose connections. Some are friends beforehand, most of them just came to watch. The visitors do not look at themselves as a group. They are somewhat distant. Their personal stories, the histories of their families, the inner and outer living conditions are not the same. They do not yet have a process as a group.

If a group stays together for longer, as in a seminar, a stronger dynamic develops. The participants create a shared experience, become part of a common story, adopt roles, experience tension. Here playback offers a possibility to work quickly with the developing conflicts, helping the group gain distance from them and incorporating them into overall group life. The stories will not be judged or evaluated. Each carries equal weight. Everyone has a right to the teller's chair. A good conductor will invite the silent people. The stories create a process, they find their theme, and they offer solutions. This creates a community in a short time.

The group dynamics are not ignored but rather are brought to a different level. They work now in the process of the stories, the pictures, and the motifs. The stories talk to each other. Primary and secondary elements communicate as if they were the figures on the stage of the group's soul. The visitors, spectators, even the tellers just watch without interfering too much. If two people have different viewpoints or feelings, both stories can be told and played and coexist.

Very important for this process to happen is the trance I was talking about earlier, the images and story trance. This slight change in the state of consciousness allows a dreamlike connection and logic. Stories answer each other and communicate like parts of a dream or like the dream and the actual life of the dreamer. There is an opportunity for the inherent tendency for wholeness.

This makes playback very helpful in the process of creating community even when there is conflict. Institutions and companies have learned this and use playback for their purposes.

One point is important to mention. We see this in "normal" playback evenings as well as in institutional settings. When people who have been quiet so far are invited to tell their story, when for example after the quick and outspoken men, the more reserved women are invited to come to the stage (or vice versa); or when in an institution the ones in not very powerful positions, like the nurses in a hospital or secretaries in an office, tell their stories, playback's power to acknowledge all sides and to fill in the missing parts will become very strong, and the spontaneity has a good chance of working. If somebody is invited to talk who is in a special situation, like Erna and Anna in our seminar, the unexpected and creative can come up.

In his book about playback theatre, Jonathan Fox tells the story of Gary who was loud and disruptive in nursery school.[17] In drama he was allowed to do exactly what was normally forbidden: he could act like an animal. This gave him and the others access to his secondary parts, his aggression and his loud voice, which were usually a disruption. So the adults could develop a new attitude, as could Gary himself.

The training allows the playback actors to be very flexible in changing roles. The spectators experience this high flexibility by just watching. The open setting also demonstrates flexibility. The visitor can see how the same person is acting as a mother, a wall, a dog, a child. This creates a playful distance and openness, facilitating the changing and taking up of new roles and attitudes, which is so difficult to do in every day life.

The very place where change happens is often the individual. The creativity of the soul lives there. The group lives through these impulses and the group can block or support them. For me this shines light on the rule that in playback the stories have to be personal stories. It sets a frame inside of which spontaneity and creativity of the soul, the dreamlike qualities in us human beings, can unfold and be held together at the same time. The teller's attitude is always his or her own involvement, it is the personal attachment: this is my story. This way the stories stay apart from each other, they don't spread into the whole group. The next teller is not caught in the story told before, but is free to find his or her own version and the possibility of a new solution.

On the other hand, "there is no such thing as independent change. The world changes, and calls us or dreams us up to fill its roles, and changes us. Or we change and touch everything in the environment. ... When a group has tried its best to work on a problem, the momentous change of one individual will change everything." But without earlier group work the individual cannot do anything. "Individual, couple and group changes happen interdependently." [18]

The many-headed group has a special chance in this process: it is not necessary that the solution is found at once. Many stories, many motifs work together and build on each other. Fritz, Richard and Ingrid are each working alone and together on answers of how to deal with loneliness and how to overcome the feeling of being a victim. And there is not only one solution, many ways can be shown. Wholeness arises only in the end, at the very end, maybe only after the end.

The same is true for an essay like this one. How playback works cannot and does not need to be explained in one article, but rather the answer will come together through the chorus of many voices, by discussing the many aspects, and by playing together.

References

Fox, J. *Acts of Service: Spontaneity, Commitment, Tradition in the Nonscripted Theatre*. New Paltz, NY: Tusitala Publishing, 1994.

Jung, C.G. *Die Dynamik des Unbewussten*, Gesammelte Werke, Bd. 8. Olten und Freiburg im Breisgau: Walter-Verlag, 1982.

Moreno, J.L. *The Essential Moreno: Writings on Spontaneity, Psychodrama and Group Method*. J. Fox, ed. New York: Springer, 1987. [*Psychodrama und Soziometrie*, herausgegeben von Jonathan Fox. Köln: Edition Humanistische Psychologie, 1989.]

Mindell, A. *River's Way—The Process Science of the Dreambody*. London: Routledge & Kegan Paul, 1985.

Mindell, A. *The Year I: Global Process Work*. London: Penguin, 1989.

Pitzele, P. "Adolescents Inside Out: Intrapsychic Psychodrama." In *Psychodrama: Inspiration and Technique*. P. Holmes and M. Karp, eds. London: Tavistock / Routledge, 1991.

Salas, J. *Improvising Real Life: Personal Story in Playback Theatre*. New Paltz, NY: Tusitala Publishing, 1993.

Notes

[1] Translated from German by the author.

[2] For more on this point, see Jo Salas, *Improvising Real Life*, 111ff.

[3] The "red thread" is a metaphor from weaving, in which a red thread allows the weaver to follow the pattern, and is a common phrase in German for 'the connecting element.' – Ed.

[4] For more on this point, see Mindell, *River's Way*, 11–29.

[5] *River's Way*, 13.

[6] *River's Way*, 25f.

[7] Fox, *Acts of Service*, 79ff.

[8] Mindell, *The Year I*, 110.

[9] *The Year I*, 97.

[10] Fox, *Acts of Service*, 32f.

[11] C.G. Jung, *Die Struktur der Seele*, Ges. Werke, Bd. 8, S. 161ff.

[12] C.G. Jung, *Allgemeine Gesichtspunkte* zur Psychologie des Traumes, Ges. Werke, Bd. 8, S. 280.

[13] Pitzele, *Adolescents*,15ff.

[14] For a discussion of playback in terms of fields, see James R. Lucal, "Emergent Drama: Renewal in Human Systems," unpublished dissertation, The Union Institute, 1995. In *The Year I*, Arnold Mindell talks about the structures that are built in groups amazingly quickly (p. 87).

[15] Mindell, *The Year I*, 89.

[16] *The Year I*, 101.

[17] Fox, *Acts of Service*, 82ff.

[18] Mindell, *The Year I*, 81

Tracing the Songlines
Searching for the Roots of Playback Theatre

Heinrich Dauber [1]

"To exist is to be perceived." [2] —*Bruce Chatwin*

"For ages storytelling has been the best form of remembering, since it is simultaneously preserving and remembering." [3] —*Harald Weinrich*

Bruce Chatwin—brilliant storyteller, talented photographer, and nomad to the core—called the mythical maps that the Australian Aborigines create to orient their walkabouts through a vast continent of time and space "songlines." For his entire life, Chatwin was a passionate "traveler," both through his own memories and through distant continents and distant times. His stories are packed with internal and external drama and at the same time always reflect the archetypal themes of humanity's search for beauty and meaning.

Songlines exist, not only in Australia, but wherever supraindividual cultural patterns of time and space intersect with personal life-patterns. The search for the source of playback theatre can be understood as an attempt to describe the hidden personal and historical roots of playback theatre as songlines.

In the Western tradition one could also say songlines appear where Lares and Penates meet. *Penates* were the family gods in Etruscan and Roman mythology (therefore representing the forebears). *Lares* were the gods of the household (therefore representing the place or the environment).

From this perspective, playback theatre forms a cultural antithesis to the anonymous electronically manipulated information society. Playback theatre, as an intimate theatre of personal stories, creates new songlines, requires the intimate participation, face-to-face, between people.[4] As teller as well as audience member, as actor as well as conductor, we contribute to the creation of new songlines, in every performance and in the whole playback theatre movement. When and where they are created is not coincidental, however, just as there are no coincidences in our personal lives or in historical contexts.

The fact that this first *academic symposium* about playback theatre takes place in the (reunified) *Germany*, seems to me—without sounding nationally arrogant or presumptuous—no more coincidental. Viewed in this light, this symposium takes place in a double *historical* and *cultural* context.

According to the unanimous assessment of various Anglo-Saxon participants in the Symposium, such an academic Symposium could not take place in the USA nor in New Zealand/Australia, because there it would not be met with comparable scientific-theoretical interest within an open academic environment. Be that as it may, three departments at the University of Kassel, Education, Social Work and Economics, were prepared to finance such a Symposium from the start; in addition, the president showed his sustained support. (Perhaps this applies exclusively to the cultural environment at Kassel, since at other German Universities theatre pedagogy courses are as a rule being dismantled.)[5] Possibly, this also reflects a distinctly Teutonic approach to art and theatre—wanting to reassure oneself epistemologically of the foundation on which one's own creative activity is actually based, and that creative expression can also be substantiated through theory, preferably with a dialectical argument in the form of a pyramid topped with a "fundamental contradiction."[6]

It is more important to recognize in this context that in the mid-nineties the German debate about the German (Nazi) past obviously changed. Various events contributed to this change in political culture: the diaries of author Victor Klemperer, composed in secret from 1933-45; Steven Spielberg's film *Schindler's List*; the debate, which was led not only in historical circles, but also in the wider public, on Daniel Goldhagen's theories presented in his book *Hitler's Willing Executioners*; but especially the exhibit presented by the Hamburg Institute for Social Research, "Crimes of the Wehrmacht;" as well as—last but not least—a remarkable debate in the *Bundestag* (German Parliament) about all these questions and topics.[7]

A representative of many Germans is the delegate of the SPD Party and Human Rights Speaker, Freimut Duve, quoted here out of the *Bundestag* minutes from the 163rd meeting on March 13, 1997:

> Last week, I was in the peculiar situation that I found the house in Osejek, in which my Jewish grandmother was picked up. I never thought—in the sixty years that I have lived—that I would ever speak to a woman who had seen this. We never thought that anyone still lived. I spoke with a woman. She described precisely how it had happened: under the protection of German soldiers. But it was Croatian Ustashas, who threw the old woman, who was disabled in her legs, into the truck. We do not know whether she died in Auschwitz or in another camp.

All of this has contributed to the fact that for some time now in Germany, after many years of making these topics taboo, the reception of stories about personal experience has grown—along with the willingness to tell them publicly. Similar cultural tendencies are shown in other countries, for example in South Africa with its Truth Commission.[8] It is no accident that in playback theatre, alongside the individual past, the collective past plays an important role. The site in Kassel in which this first academic symposium on playback took place is the renovated iron-foundry of the Henschel factory, which produced locomotive engines and tanks for the Nazis in the war; because of this factory, Kassel was firebombed by the allies. As a result, more than 40,000 people died in one night. This location is very symbolic, and many participants made sympathetic references towards it.

In addition, there is another societal reason for the growing interest in personal stories. While individuals live socially more and more isolated lives, and community-building rituals have almost disappeared in modern industrialized society, a historically new interest in personally experienced stories has formed. This is the case for districts establishing history workshops, and for institutions such as nursing-homes, with their conversation-circles, as well as for larger institutions and wider political changes connected to the political and economic bonds which are bringing peoples together around the world.[9]

Should this assessment prove correct, around the end of this century a cultural wave of personal stories will approach us—who might be readier than the playback theatre movement? Is it prepared to take on this challenge and the moral, educational, political, and artistic responsibility connected with it?

Playback's Roots

Songlines form where collective and individual life patterns intersect, in the "chatter every evening between *Lares* and *Penates*." [10] In the search for playback theatre's songlines, it seems interesting and worthwhile to get closer to Jonathan Fox and Jo Salas's common history—on a long walk or over a glass of wine. I have discovered this much about songlines:

In the biographies of Jonathan Fox and Jo Salas, two contemporary movements of the seventies come together: on the one hand, the culture of political resistance, as expressed through "pedagogy of liberation" and the connected fight against the "culture of silence" (Freire);[11] on the other, the search for alternatives to the consumer society of mass-produced goods and services, for a simpler, more "convivial" community-oriented lifestyle (Illich).[12] Both of these movements greatly influenced the original development of playback theatre and its political and moral character.[13]

Freire views the "teacher" and the "student" as partners in a dialogue about reality, the structure of which is reflected in the individual and collective consciousness. Fox extends this framework around the conductor, storyteller, actor, and audience member. The goal remains the same—a dialogue about individual experience, which leads to decoding (and changing) commonly experienced reality. In Freire's concept this process is attempted through pedagogical means, while in playback theatre this is carried out more implicitly than explicitly.

Illich's criticism refers to the modern context of alienation, in which experts and institutions decide which "needs" people have and how to satisfy them. Fox extends this criticism to include modern theatre. Playback theatre does not have a traditional "audience." The members of the audience are invited to become tellers of their own experiences in their own words in a community-building ritual.

In the eyes of its founder playback does not wear the hat of the Californian ego-trippers, with their culture of fun. Nor is it allied to the creative performance coaching method practiced in modern organizations, much less a "theatre sport," in which groups spontaneously compete against each other.

Playback theatre is neither therapeutic theatre nor social work. It is neither shamanic therapy nor theatre of the oppressed. Perhaps it is a bit of all of these. The original songlines of playback are made up of the conjunction of the *Penates* of Jonathan and Jo's families with *Lares* from all over the world. They combined these to compose the first playback theatre songline—rhythm. Obviously, New Zealand's *Lares* play a special part, not only because Jo Salas was born in New Zealand and Jonathan Fox met her there, but also because apparently in New Zealand (differently from in Australia) a special tradition has grown and been maintained, in which their own past as a colonial frontier state as well as that of the native Maori culture is treated with respect. Therefore, they continue to keep their collective memory alive, despite the fundamental differences in their cultural roots.[14]

That playback theatre—especially in the USA and Germany—is connected with psychodrama, is evidenced by Jonathan Fox's professional background (he edited Moreno's collected writings), and playback's publications and reviews, several of which have appeared in psychodrama publications.[15] Jonathan Fox and Jo Salas certainly bore the stamp of their personal histories (New York, Nepal, New Zealand) and education[16] before they became involved in therapeutic practice (Jonathan for a brief period, Jo over many years as a music therapist).

Intellectually, from the perspective of collective songlines within a European/North American context, playback theatre stems (like psychodrama, gestalt therapy and theme-centered interaction) from the magic triangle of Vienna-Berlin-Frankfurt, which produced countless social, cultural, political and philosophical innovations during the period lasting from the turn of the century to the beginning of the Nazi terror. The representatives of this ferment—Jacob Levy Moreno, Fritz Perls, Martin

Buber, Kurt Lewin, Erich Fromm, and Ruth Cohn—only to name a few, valued each other highly and learned from each other. As Jews, socialists, and radical humanists, they were forced to emigrate. Subsequently, in Germany their ideas and political-artistic-pedagogical concepts were buried in oblivion for almost fifty years, until the late seventies, when some were reimported from America, most commonly in the form of therapeutic methods.[17]

As part of the generation that was born during the war, it took me many years to fathom the wealth of people and ideas which were irretrievably lost from Germany and Europe as a result of the Nazis' criminal policies. I have often mourned this deeply.[18] I wonder if the Jewish heritage of Jonathan Fox and Jo Salas (as well as other speakers and participants at the Symposium in Kassel) is meaningful in the search for playback theatre's songlines. Besides the central question in the Jewish religion and philosophy, "How can we counteract forgetting?" it seems to me that an internationally cosmopolitan education which was nourished by European Jewish heritage, and which according to Hannah Arendt, grew out of a "position outside-any-societal-restraints" led to a fully nonprejudiced behavior.[19]

Jonathan Fox was obviously always fascinated by this Berlin-Vienna-Frankfurt magical triangle of the twenties and thirties. (Perhaps that is where his first interest in Moreno arose.) In 1920 in *Schriften des Vaters* (later, *Words of the Father*), Moreno anonymously published "Die Reihe der reinen Örter I" [The Series of Pure Places], a text on *Stegreiftheater*, with the subtitle, "Invitation to an Encounter." [20]

Nevertheless, Fox—similar to Paul Goodman amongst others (myself included)—is not from the direct lineage of this generation, but perhaps in Goethe's sense of *Wahlverwandtschaften* [literally 'chosen relations'], he is a "grand-nephew by choice." It remains for future research[21] to document the development of this partly underground, partly purposely buried tradition. Fox himself showed in a historical essay about Moreno's *Stegreiftheater* in New York, how this tradition, at least indirectly, was influenced by the post-revolutionary Russian theatre movement called the "Blue Blouses." [22] Such seeds, via the intermedial station of the Living Newspaper, became psychodrama.

In Europe, especially in Germany, this tradition continued after the

Second World War with Hilarion Petzold, and among others, the Russian in Paris Vladamir Iljine, a psychotherapist and psychoanalyst from the school of the Hungarian psychoanalyst Ferenczi. Petzold, like Fox, was also trained by the Morenos and later founded the so-called "Integrated Therapy." [23]

These few examples only outline the larger context in which playback theatre was "invented" by Jonathan Fox. At a glance it is clear how inappropriate it would be to define playback—or other recent forms of this tradition, such as gestalt pedagogy—as directly related to forms of therapy (in this case, to psychodrama). Whoever is active in this scene today, is culturally, and often also through personal experience, anchored in a broad and varied tradition.

The Historical Challenge

Right at the beginning of the first meeting of German-speaking playback theatre groups in Bad Bevensen in 1996, a woman from Berlin told the following story. While visiting an exhibit in the newly opened Centrum Judaicum in Berlin, she stood in front of a photo of a little girl in the window of a house, which, before the war, was located across from the museum. The house was now gone. Only the photo of this (Jewish) child remained. While she reflected on what had happened to the girl, an older American visitor entered the room, looked around and went straight towards the photo. Without explaining himself further, he gestured to the photo and said quietly, "I knew her."

Everyone present was deeply moved by this story. One of the first comments about it was, "How can we recover the cultural heritage which we have lost? Could it be that the spread of playback theatre in Germany is a part of our own tradition returning back?"

This brings up two corresponding questions, which are as speculative as they are fascinating: What would have become of today's Europe, if these traditions had not been lost almost two generations ago? And what would have become of America without the influence of the scientists, artists, and authors who fled Europe?

The history of Germany, Europe, and America cannot be undone. Nevertheless, precisely out of this reciprocal, multifaceted, interconnected heritage grows the historical challenge: for the German-speaking area, to become conscious of our own cultural roots and to reclaim the lost humanitarian traditions; for the USA, to critically account for the foundation of its own cultural modernization.

In addition, there is a third challenge, not just valid for Europe and the USA, but a truly global challenge: to preserve humanity's common cultural heritage, which does not only consist of worldwide information networks. This applies especially to the linkage with pre-electronic 'songlines' and preliterary forms of collective cultural self-reflection. Only when we are able to know and express where we come from will we be able to understand where we need to go. Museums, history exhibits, and theatre and concert performances could contribute much to the formation of such a historical consciousness. The stories told in playback theatre are the most alive form of such individual and collective self-reflection that I know: Playback mobilizes the whole person, and allows one to form thoughts, feelings, and impressions in a bodily expression that connects individual and collective experiences in a unique way.

What Bruce Chatwin reported about the songs of the Australian Aborigines can also apply to the stories told in playback theatre: "A man's verses were his title deeds to territory. He could lend them to others. He could borrow other verses in return. The one thing he couldn't do was sell or get rid of them." [24]

Notes

[1] Translated from German by the author.

[2] Chatwin, Bruce, *The Songlines* (London: Jonathan Cape, 1987), 14.

[3] Weinrich, Harald, in *Spiegel* (No. 20, 1997), 192; compare to Lethe, *Kunst und Kritik des Vergessen*, (Munich: C.H. Beck, 1997).

[4] See Mardorf, Elisabeth, *Das kann doch kein Zufall sein! Verblüffende Ereignisse und geheimnisvolle Fügungen in unserem Leben* (Munich: Koesel, 1997).

[5] The Kassel *Documenta X*, a major European art event, took place in 1997.

[6] Compare this to the essay by Johann Galtung, "*Kultur und intellektueller Stil: ein vergleichender Essay über sachsonische, teutonische, gallische und nipponische Wissenschaft*" (Freie Universität Berlin, 1983).

[7] Compare to the interview with Jan Philipp Reemtsma, "Die Skala des Scheußlichen ist nach unten offen," *Frankfurter Rundschau* (April 14, 1997), 7. Also compare to the so-called Goldhagen debate in the *Themenheft der Zeitschrift Psyche* (51. Jg., vol. 6), as well as

the included article by Margarete Mitscherlich, "Erinnern, Wiederholen und Durcharbeiten," in reference to Daniel Jonah Goldhagen's book, *Hitlers willige Vollstrecker [Hitler's Willing Executioners]*, 479-493.

[8] Compare to various critical contributions about the Truth Commission's work in *Querbrief* (Berlin: Weltfriedensdienst 1/1997).

[9] For example, at the International Women's Conference in China in 1995, an international playback women's team, consisting of players from the USA, Japan, Australia, New Zealand, England, and Switzerland, offered altogether ten performances and three workshops.

[10] "If you listen carefully, especially at night, in the houses of Leandra, you will hear them whispering on, talking over one another, cajoling, bellowing and giggling." From Italo Calvino's *Die unsichtbaren Städte* (*Invisible Cities*) (Munich: Hanser, 1977), 93.

[11] Paulo Freire died on May 2, 1997, in Sao Paulo, his home city, just before the Playback Symposium. In the early eighties, he occasionally visited the GhK (Kassel University). The PT Symposium was dedicated to his memory.

[12] Illich would have spoken of "vernacular speech" and "convivial necessities of life."

[13] In shaping the original playback theatre, Jonathan Fox had planned—in his own words—to critically analyze Moreno with Illich and Freire!

[14] See the Maori song that opens Fe Day's essay.

[15] See Jonathan Fox, "Playback Theatre: The Community Sees Itself," in *Drama in Therapy*, G. Schattner & R. Courtney, eds. (New York: Drama Book Specialists, 1981); Fox, "*Die inszenierte persönliche Geschichte im Playback Theater*," *Psychodrama*, 1 (June 1991), 31-44.

[16] Jonathan Fox studied literature, sociology, and experimental theatre; Jo Salas studied music and art. With these backgrounds, their reference system for the foundation of playback theatre defines the independent form (of theatre/art): for Fox, the literary theatre, for Salas, the arts.

[17] See Heinrich Dauber, *Grundlagen Humanistischer Pädagogik: Integrative Ansätze zwischen Therapie und Politik* (Bad Heilbrunn: Klinkhardt, 1997).

[18] As a very young man, I belonged to one of the first groups of German volunteers who participated in work camps in Israeli kibbutzim in the early sixties. Thirty years later, as I tried to discover, in an arduous roundabout way, who the people were who took us in without resentment, I found out that they were the former students of the elite educators of Germany before WW II.

[19] Hannah Arendt, *Ich will verstehen*, (Munich: Piper, 1996), 64.

[20] Anonymous, 'Exlibris Ignatii Gentges,' *Verlag des Vaters* (Potsdam & Berlin: Gustav Keipenheuer Verlag, 1920). Obviously a theatre board member or critic, Hans Knudsen reacted to the article in the magazine *Die Szene, Blätter für Bühnenkunst*, published by the Vereinigung künstlerischer Bühnenvorstände (XIV.1924), 156f. There it says: "In the countless rows of suggested reforms of the German theatre, this one was missing; and one cannot wonder in the least according to recent experience, when not a single good hair remains of the old theatre, and the reforms come exclusively from improvised theatre. The directing of improvisation is, of course, entirely different from the directing of historical theatre. Theatre painters and hairdressers also affect the audience, in which all the previous stages contribute to the miracle of conception and birth. In this way an anecdotal occurrence can be translated into living theatre…"

[21] In his autobiography, the future-researcher Robert Jungk reported on his mother's activities in Berlin in the twenties: With the cabaret artist and social-critic Charly Röllinghof, she founded "Berlin's first *Stegreiftheater* on Kurfürstendamm. A task which fit her now rather corpulent body to a T. Namely, there she did not have to memorize and recite long texts that others had written, rather she could say what she wanted, her own thoughts. This resurrection of the old theatre form of 'Commedia dell'Arte' immediately attracted the innovation-loving Berlin. The catchphrase, 'Every evening a première,' drew the public as much as the challenge: 'You decide the theme yourself.' In fact, the five or six comedians, who had come together to take on this risk, never knew before the performance what the theme would be this time. As soon as the curtain rose, someone from the audience would call out a current issue or name, and the fun would begin.

I can only remember one of these improvised performances precisely. On this evening, my mother played a resolute fifty-year-old woman, the wife of the 'iron Gustav,' who at that time was one of the most popular people in Berlin. He was travelling by his old carriage then from the Spree to the Seine as a gesture of peace and understanding, a trip which, due to the old-fashioned form of transportation, took an unusually long time, also because the hero was celebrated with much schnapps and beer and apéritifs in every town he rolled through, so much so that he often had trouble finding his way back to the carriage. While Gustav slept off his drunkenness, his wife sat neglected in Berlin and cursed and swooned with yearning, despaired, sang, and threw tantrums. Mama was great at this, and I saw an entirely new side of her. But after a few weeks, the improvisation proved too strenuous. In addition, Berlin was hunting for new sensations, and the *Stegreiftheater* found less and less attendance." Robert Jungk, *Trotzdem—Mein Leben für die Zukunft,* (Munich: Knaur, 1994), 56f.

[22] Jonathan Fox, "Morenos Stegreiftheater in New York," in *Jahrbuch für Psychodrama, psychosoziale Praxis and Gesellschaftspolitk* (Opladen, 1994), 7-17.

[23] See Vladimir Iljine, Hilarion Petzold & Ina Schmidt, "Didaktisches théâtre permanent in der Erwachsenenbildung," in *Volkshochschule im Westen* (Cologne, 2, 1972), 28-29; as well as Hilarion Petzold, *Theater oder Spiel des Lebens*, (Frankfurt: Verlag für Humanistische Psychologie, 1982).

[24] Bruce Chatwin, *The Songlines* (London: Jonathan Cape, 1987), 57.

Playback Portrait

FUSAKO KATO
Japan

Fusako Kato, born in 1942, is currently the director of two day treatment centers and one group home residence. The members' diagnosis is varied, but they share an inability to function in the everyday world. She was a pioneer in her region for rejecting the typical "skill development" approach to rehabilitation in favor of an emphasis on human rights and quality of life for the "members" (not "clients") under her charge.

She first invited a playback theatre company, PlaybackAZ, to come to her group home three years ago after seeing a performance. They have been coming monthly ever since. To what benefit? Fusako Kato, known as Chako, produces a carefully written outline: "The members' self-image is very low. But through telling their stories with PT," she says, pointing to her paper, "the members find respect, sympathy, consideration, and acceptance."

At first they were very timid, Chako explains. They could not tell stories intelligibly, join in as actors, or express their feelings fully. But little by little they opened up. Their faces became more cheerful and they started to laugh a lot. Their stories became easier to understand. Some of them became interested in acting. One woman who does not usually communicate clearly likes to act in fluid sculptures. It is a big surprise to watch her when she expresses the exact essence of tellers' words. At first the PT team conducted workshops with the members, but now for the most part they lean towards a performance format, in spite of the interest of some members in acting. "There is more cure this way," she adds, "because it is not so complicated." Members can simply be tellers, not tellers *and* actors.

A secondary benefit concerns staff members (present at the PT sessions), some of whom are former members in day treatment. She describes one worker, for example, who kept running away because he couldn't stand the pressure of his new staff status. After sharing his feeling in a story in PT before other members of the community, however, he received much sympathy and acceptance, and his running away has stopped. Another staff member, who made the jump from member to staff eight years ago, had a big problem with anger. Playback theatre has helped him feel OK about expressing negative feelings, says Chako.

When asked if her superiors were supportive of her bringing PT to her group home, Chako answers, "I'm the boss!" Obviously there is no question of her right to introduce something innovative and different. She adds that now other directors are showing interest since she introduced PT at a staff development meeting.

After three years Chako has gotten close to some of the playback theatre colleagues, and has started studying PT herself.

How do I know who or where I am until I hear what I say?

Fe Day

Kia whakarongo ake au ki te tangi a te manu nei
a te maatui
tui tui tuituia
tuia i runga
tuia i raro
tuia i roto
tuia i waho
tuia i te here tangata
i takea mai i Hawaiki nui, Hawaiki roa, Hawaiki pamamao
ka rongo te po
ka rongo te ao

Let me always listen
to the cry of the bird - tui - weaving
weaving together what is above
what is below
what is inside
what is outside

weaving the mooring-line of people
that originated in the great Homeland
the long Homeland, the Homeland far away
the darkness hears/senses/feels
the light hears/senses/feels

These words of a traditional Maori incantation bring the indigenous language of my home, Aoteraroa/New Zealand, into this publication. Another purpose of mine in using them is to facilitate our thinking of the other levels of reality that always lap within and around us as we think and work together. So often in international business/professional culture (that amorphous omnipresent culture located somewhere between a boardroom and a helicopter), these dimensions of our meeting together go unrecognized. Of course, these are levels of being that playback theatre acknowledges and enables people to activate. Still, by referring to them at this point, I am invoking a kind of protection for myself and for you, the reader, as well.

So, I place myself in this discussion as a Pakeha/European New Zealander. This is not a simple position. The two words, "Maori," meaning the indigenous people of Aotearoa/New Zealand, and "Pakeha," meaning people of European descent in Aotearoa, are terms which came into being when the two groups of people encountered each other.

> Prior to the advent of Europeans Maori people had no single term for themselves. People were distinguished from one another by their tribal names, but with the coming of the whalers, sealers and traders, the word Pakeha was used to designate the strangers. The word is derived from pakepakeha or pakehakeha, "imaginary beings resembling men [sic] with fair skins." The word 'maori' means 'normal', 'usual', or 'ordinary', which through usage has become capitalized to refer to the Maori people collectively.[1]

So our ancestors named themselves in relation to one another! Moreover, I experience the Pakeha part of me very much in relation to Maori people, issues, and language, in deeply rewarding and sometimes challenging ways.

The European part of me is also complex, and I expect that many European-descent inhabitants of what were (are?) colonies experience the love/hate relationship I have lived through with regard to Europe. As a child, the incantations that accompanied me through the New Zealand landscape were lines of English poetry. I could draw a map of the High Street in Oxford because my mother had so often drawn us a map with a fork, on the tablecloth at dinner, to accompany some story of her hometown. I lived over and over again the journeys of my father when as a prisoner of war in Italy he escaped over the Dolomites into Switzerland. Later I married into a family of Hungarian Jews who continue to inhabit New Zealand as if it were somewhere just out of Budapest. Yet, while loving Europe in some ways, I remain distinct. When I am in Europe, I am definitely *not* a European.

There are many other ways I could position myself, many other systems of classification I could use. I am positioned as woman, mother, sole parent, lesbian; as a person of middle class origin; as a member of the helping professions; an educator. I have chosen to elucidate the placing of myself as regards geography, culture, ancestry because that is to me the potential of a "gathering in thought" such as this book (and, indeed of a playback theatre performance)—that people from very different "places" of all kinds can be visible and be heard. All of these positions influence what I want to say about our practice of Playback. These are *my* truths, not *the* truth!

Theory is OK

Playback can be viewed from many theoretical viewpoints, and in fact to begin to talk about it at all we have to use a theoretical template. However, our society often discourages us from becoming aware of what kind of theory we are applying to discussions of our activities (in New Zealand certainly). Again, we are deeply saturated in certain kinds of theoretical viewpoints, expressed in the media, in our professional disciplines, and in other discourses we engage in. Often the hardest thing to identify is the theory one is most deeply imbued with. Another complication for us as playback practitioners is that I suspect many of us are strongly kinesthetic learners and operators. Perhaps we have to be in order to be drawn to the work in the first place. Therefore we operate strongly in our bodies, in movement, and in action. The idea of theory may be one that comes quite strangely to us.

Yet, everything we do expresses a theory, what the *Concise Oxford Dictionary* calls "a supposition or system of ideas explaining something." For what you see when you look at something depends on what kind of window you look out of. Often it is very difficult to see the shape of your window when you are looking out of it. It is only when you can get some distance and look back at it that you gain an idea of its shape. This essay is an attempt on my part to do just that and to offer you the chance to do so as well.

I have found it very helpful to put theory into three main groupings, which I have gratefully taken from my colleague at the Auckland Institute of Technology, Mary Melrose. In her chapter, "Got a Philosophical Match? Does it Matter?" in Ortrun Zuber-Skerrit's *New Directions in Action Research*, Melrose focuses on "three paradigms—functional, transactional, and critical—and their underlying philosophical bases, commonly recognized in many fields of education, including educational research, program development, program evaluation and educational leadership." (I am aware that I am using here paradigms of educational theory.) Few of us would dispute the important educational dimension of playback workshops and performances. As an educator involved in playback, I have found such an exploration productive and a helpful contrast to the perhaps more common psychology- or aesthetics-based approach to theorizing about our work in playback. In any case, these paradigm groupings can be identified in many other discourses. I am hoping that it will be useful to look at these three paradigms and highlight what are some of the key emphases and questions that each gives rise to in terms of playback development and practice. It seems to me clear that when we come together to talk about playback, we do so often through the functional/technical and transactional/interpretist paradigms, as I will outline below. While acknowledging the usefulness of these ways of seeing and describing, I would like to go on to explore what insights the critical/emancipatory paradigm can bring to our work.

The functional, also known as the technical or logical positivist, paradigm, values "concrete and factual bodies of technical knowledge and generalizations" in a curriculum "based on previous 'moral' curriculum codes which trained 'the masses' for their duties to the state and which produced highly skilled workers to assist the economy." Leadership in this paradigm is hierarchical and is likely to value efficiency in terms of the present goals and values of an institution.

In the functional paradigm we will be asking things like, What is playback? How should it be done? When we do playback training we will be "reproductive, technical, task- and skills-based..." [2]

In the transactional/interpretist paradigm we will be looking at individuals and asking about their values and interpretations of the world. Leaders in this paradigm will "practice negotiation and encourage... development to maximize contributions to the team."

We will be concerned chiefly with such things as, Who are the individuals doing playback? What attitudes and values are we expressing? When we train performers or engage in discussion of playback, our work will be "based on the needs of the individual students or group... process, rather than product-orientated... people-centered..."

Critical theory, however, creates a paradigm that asks different kinds of questions. It was a situation full of irony and significance for me to talk about critical theory at the University in Kassel, which is so close to where the group of writers who originated critical theory worked (at the Institute of Social Research at the University of Frankfurt, founded in 1923). Horkheimer, Adorno, and Marcuse were the best known members of this school. However, "it is vital to grasp that there is no such thing as unified critical theory. Rather, there are critical theories." [3] Critical theory is intensely interested in theory itself and in unearthing the hidden theory in actions and practices. It rejects the idea of 'naturalness' or 'human nature' and scrutinizes the situations in which such statements are made to see whether the views of one group are dominating over those of others. It is concerned above all with emancipation. It critiques the obsession of industrialized societies with "efficiency" and has named it "instrumental rationality" which it sees as "the dominant feature of the modern world. It is the feature that most requires criticism and challenge, the feature from whose malformations and constraints we need emancipation... Instrumental rationality limits itself to 'How to do it?' questions rather than 'Why do it?' or 'Where are we going?' questions." In the critical paradigm, we will be looking at groups of individuals and asking ourselves and each other: What is *happening* in a playback performance? How does it relate to social change? How can we critique it? Our discussions will be "based on visions of a better, fairer world… asking critical questions, shaking previously held beliefs, querying current systems, acting as change agent." [4]

Let me place myself within the critical paradigm and begin by asking, What is happening in a playback performance? In answering this question, I want to focus particularly on three of the myriad of answers that could be given to this question.

First, *someone is talking and other people are listening*. Does it matter who talks? Who tells? It is my contention that it matters *very much*, because the chance to tell one's story is part of what a playback theatre performance has to offer.

Imagine Your Ancestor

I would like to ask you to take some time and think about the life of an ancestor of yours who was born in the nineteenth century. Particularly think, if you will, of the role of speech and personal communication in that person's life. (Whichever gender you have chosen, now add a person of the other sex so that now you are considering the lives of both a man and a woman.) Give some time to thinking about different times of day when the family or community gathered. What kinds of things are happening?

Now think of your own family and community. What similarities do you see with how things were 100 years ago? What differences? It seems clear, doesn't it, that in the atomized industrial setting, opportunities to present our accounts of ourselves and our lives have been drastically reduced? People strenuously resist this erosion and continue to exchange narratives: indeed it is one of our main needs because in the communion that comes with sharing our stories all kinds of healing may take place. In any workplace or gathering, people negotiate their own network of people to whom they can tell their stories. This is the informal knitting together of any enterprise that often goes completely unregarded and unvalued.

However, many people certainly live without the sense of a hearth, a campfire, a meeting house or communal space within which individual stories can be told and heard. This may represent a much more serious attack on our humanness than we have yet fully registered. We are denied the chance to experience individual and group catharsis, that crisis of pity and fear. In fact the most common experiences of catharsis in many contemporary settings may be in the dehumanized disembodied arena of the information media and electronic technology. We experience ourselves as individuals alone or in darkness, hiding our reactions from each other.

What a contrast this is to earth-based communal cultures where, as Rose Pere, a Maori educator and thinker, writes in a section headed "Whatumanawa" (the emotional aspect):

> Sustenance and an understanding of the individual and the family as a whole is considered important. Children are encouraged to express their emotions so that the people who are involved with the parenting know how to support, encourage and guide the children. Crying for joy or sadness by both sexes is regarded as natural and healthy by the Maori. This form of expression is not regarded as a weakness. Emotional involvement and interaction are regarded as important meeting points for human beings.[5]

An important addition is that, by losing communal venues for speaking and being heard, we also lose the chance to experience the clash and renegotiation of cultures in a group small enough for us to humanly manage.

Each person "as a positioned subject, grasps certain human phenomena better than others. He or she occupies a position or structural location and observes with a particular angle of vision..." [6] Yet, without the chance to speak and externalize the insights that emerge from our angle of vision, we are unable to experience our own positioning, far less to make any sort of comparison or negotiation with other people who are positioned differently. Without the disjunction and disruption that comes from hearing those who are not like ourselves, we are never able to gain a picture of who in fact we are and what structural location we see and speak from. For "all interpretations are provisional; they are made by positioned subjects who are prepared to know certain things and not others." [7] The hope is that a playback performance will open up the repertoire of the things the audience members are "prepared to know."

In terms of our practice of playback then, these insights lead us to particularly value the time during which members of the audience talk to each other; the greatest diversity possible in the tellers; participation of as many people as possible in the performance rather than the domination of the performance by a certain group or type of people. The conductor needs to develop a sense of the subgroups in the audience and the society and to nourish an awareness of the kinds of people so far represented by the tellers who have volunteered. The conductor indicates how inclusive or exclusive the world of the performance will be.

A second thing that is happening in a playback performance is that *narratives are being enacted upon the body*. Tellers often present half-formed and tentative formulations of their own feeling and experience. To tell is one step, involving their own use of the language available to them. Then to see the narrative expanded, through a deepened use of language, characterization, sound and movement, allows them to gain another kind of understanding, as they apprehend elements and aspects of the story which they have not seen before.

This is a moment in which critical theory also has insights to offer. Michel Foucault's concern "to show how power was 'inscribed on the body' can best be understood by considering his notions of surveillance and sexuality." He described Jeremy Bentham's model prison, the Panopticon, in which each "prisoner is totally, permanently visible to an observer who is himself unseen" [8] and suggested that Western society has extended this disciplinary system into the fabric of daily life with its introjected obsession about measuring, comparing, and surveying our bodies and ourselves. Here, the playback company can also explode and evade the discipline which surveillance in the form of stereotypes and rigid aesthetic expectations has placed upon the body in our time and in many of the industrialized countries we come from. We are able to reclaim a ritual space of enactment and incantation which subverts the tendency of the Western industrialized state to pass everything (especially those things to do with the body) "through the endless mill of speech."

This point will lead us in our practice to positively value different body shapes, abilities and disabilities, ages and capacities, emphasizing physical and fitness training, to encourage daring, skilled, and audacious expressiveness in all performers and to critically disrupt stereotypes of "dance" or "the beautiful."

Honoring Complexity

Thirdly, *representations of the world are being made*. To make them, the actors bring not only their performance skills but also all of their knowledge, hunches, heartbreaks, and illuminations.

We often say that we are going for the "essence" of a story. Yet, even (especially?) in saying that, we have to make sure that we are not de-politicizing the narrative and turning it into a myth that "abolishes the complexity of human acts... does away with all dialectics, with any going back beyond what is immediately visible, organizes a world that is without contradictions because it is without depth..." [9]

We have all seen playback enactments like this and I know I have even (occasionally) been part of them, though I hate to admit it! Recently, I was part of a performance focussing on harassment in the workplace where I am employed. The first really effective fluid sculpture was when a teller told of the way the people who are privileged in the hierarchy impose their views of the world on everyone else. The actors (community members who had received minimal training) simply repeated the teller's words in rather lusterless impersonal ways and imprecise, wavy movements. Then one of them took the bold step of enacting the leaders who were not only putting forward a bland view of events but also suppressing the other views. A large, beautiful woman, she simply started sitting on the other actors. They were amazed and so was the audience. Then the moment took off in gales of laughter, as the audience recognized the truth of what she was suggesting—the contradiction between the bland, patronizing words being used and the oblivious suppression actually being carried out. By going for the contradiction she had got us straight into the deep story with all its contradictions and energy. It is true that, playback being an imperfect art, sometimes the story seems to elude us and become even less in the retelling. Yet, if we can find in the story the contradictions that give it its internal conflict, we will find our way to its drama, paradox, and richness. I would contend it is possible for us to learn to read these contradictions if we are willing to challenge ourselves and each other to read the contradictions in the worldviews we are being presented with and are presenting.

To do this, we need to positively value our own and our playback company's internal contradictions. And we need to seek company members with divergent worldviews as well as developed performance skills. To be a playback theatre actor is sometimes challenging for professional theatre practitioners, perhaps because it is configured not so much in the model of the skilled luminary but more in that of the "citizen actor, who performs as needed by the community, then melts back into the social fabric..." [10]

As I look at playback theatre, a key question from the critical theoretical paradigm is, "How does this (the performance) relate to social change?" My sense is that playback is as related to social change as the practitioners performing it are. It is possible to perform playback satisfyingly within the transactional/intepretist paradigm in which individuals' ideas and interpretations of the world will be explored. Many practitioners with an interest in aesthetics will site their performances in this worldview. Yet it is equally possible to perform playback in the context of social concerns and social change and to do this with no less commitment to the highest possible artistic standards.

The 1997 International Playback Theatre Conference in Perth located itself fair and square in the territory of this question by its conference theme, Cultural Diversity. At that conference, I coordinated an afternoon discussion about ways in which the playback theatre forms can be made to relate more explicitly to social change. I was curious to hear from anyone using Boal's Theatre of the Oppressed techniques in conjunction with playback, as we in Auckland sometimes have. When there is a story where clearly the teller has been and feels oppressed, we gain their permission to re-enact the story, with, this time, the option for anyone in the audience to break the enactment by saying "stop" and then to suggest new strategies to the teller. (No other character may be instructed to behave differently, but they do react differently to the new behaviors of the teller.) We have only ever used this method in commissioned performances, but as a conductor, it is an option I value having. It enables us to very explicitly introduce the idea of social change. For the most part, playback's relationship with this idea is oblique and subtle. However, I would suggest it is no less powerful for that—*if* (and sometimes it seems a big if) the company is aware of the social stresses and sites of struggle in its own society, and is prepared to be in conscious relationship with them and not be afraid to bring out the harsh realities embodied in many of our stories.

Also at Perth, an experiment was carried out in one of the conference sessions of doing a PT scene by making present in the action many of the social groupings which impacted on the story. I watched spellbound and yet deeply concerned as I observed the figure of the teller becoming more and more diminished by the complex canvas surrounding her. I observed a greater and greater engagement by the conductor in the fascinating internal structure of the story and a diminishing of the conductor's awareness of the teller. This represented to me a serious breach of the contract made with the audience in a playback performance, which is that tellers will be cared for responsibly by both the conductor and by other audience members.

I feel we, as a community, are in process with this aspect of playback. More and more I have come to see that if we have actors from diverse communities working in companies, and if we mandate those company members to explore together the different ways in which we see power, control, suppression, emancipation, then we will be able to bring these elements of our lives and knowing into our work. We will see these forms of literacy and self awareness as being just as valid as currently we value emotional/social competence and artistic skill.

A final key question is, "How can we critique what happens in a playback theatre performance?" The answer to this is short—by *wanting* to. We need to want to find ways to continue to critically reflect on what we are doing and to keep pushing ourselves to take on board the need to be engaged in social and political dialogue with ourselves, each other, our audiences, and our world. If we do this, if the actors and musicians *will*, if the conductor succeeds in creating an environment in which personal safety and group exploration can occur, then playback theatre has the potential to be a profoundly humane theatre form, subverting the categories imposed on people by an increasingly authoritarian and invasive economic hegemony. In seeing how they are positioned and have been constructed, tellers take possession of their own narratives; they, their communities and we, their performers, escape, even for a short time, but with promises of potential emancipation hinted at, from the rigid dehumanizing ersatz narratives of popular culture. We emerge as neither consumers nor customers but citizens of the world, with our own sense of power and agency.

I have given you an idea of some of the things I think are going on in a playback performance. To do this I have used the insights of critical theory, "a mode of thought which never loses sight of the question, 'What is it *for*?' and which acknowledges values, moral problems, and consequences in every aspect of human conduct and its study." [11] I have explored some ideas of what all of this may have to do with social change and tried to encourage all of us to continue to critique our work in this way.

References

Barthes, R. *Mythologies*. London: Paladin, 1973.

Foucault, M. *The History of Sexuality: Vol 1: An Introduction*. London: Tavistock, 1979.

Fox, J. *Acts of Service: Spontaneity, Commitment, Tradition in the Nonscripted Theatre*. New Paltz, N.Y: Tusitala Publishing, 1994.

Gibson, R. *Critical Theory and Education*. London: Hodder and Stoughton, 1986.

Rosaldo, R. *Culture and Truth the Remaking of Social Analysis*. Boston: Beacon Press, 1989.

Walker, R. *Ka Whawhai Tonu Matou—Struggle Without End*. Auckland: Penguin Books, 1990.

Ywhahoo, D. *Voices of Our Ancestors*. Boston: Shambhala, 1987.

Zuber-Skerritt, O. *New Directions in Action Research*. London: Falmer Press, 1996.

Notes

1 Walker, *Struggle*, 94.

2 See Melrose in Zuber-Skerritt, *New Directions*, 50, 53-61.

3 Gibson, *Critical Theory*, 3.

4 *Critical Theory*, 7.

5 Pere, R., "*Te Wheke: Whaia te Matauranga me te Aroha*," in S. Middleton, ed., *Women and Education in Aotearoa* (Wellington: Port Nicholson Press, 1988), 17. 'Whatumanawa' literally means 'the eye [whatu] of the heart [manawa].'

6 Rosaldo, *Culture and Truth*, 19.

7 *Culture and Truth*, 8.

8 Gibson, *Critical Theory*, 132.

9 Barthes, *Mythologies*, 156.

10 Fox, *Acts of Service*, 214.

11 Gibson, *Critical Theory*, 35.

Practical Aspects from the Life of a Playback Theatre Ensemble

Marlies Arping and Daniel Feldhendler [1]

In this article we will report on selected aspects of the four-year development of our playback theatre ensemble, from its founding in September 1993 until the time of the Symposium at Kassel University in May 1997.

In the first part, we introduce the formation of the *Spiegelbühne Frankfurt Playback Theatre* and explain some of our conceptual ideas preceding this foundation. In the second part, a retrospective by the founding leaders, we will summarize important moments in the life of the ensemble and further describe phases in the group's development process. In addition, we will show how group life was influenced both by various workshops and by external events from members' personal lives and society on the whole.

The *Spiegelbühne* Frankfurt Playback Theatre has existed since the beginning of September 1993. We began with seven members (four women and three men), including two married couples (the two leaders and two group members). An additional man came to the second rehearsal, and after two months of rehearsing, another woman joined us.

Of these nine members, seven had had various amounts of previous experience with playback theatre (PT)—either as participants at workshops or as members of PT groups. In January of 1995, in the middle of our second year, we took on two additional members (one woman and one man). They had become familiar with the work of the ensemble by attending performances and brought some of their own previous experience from earlier PT workshops.

We ourselves began our PT work as founding leaders following a training program with Jonathan Fox in 1988, and since then have both continually worked as group members and as conductors with a number of groups. In addition, we were able to augment our experience by participating in various PT workshops and international conferences. In the summer of 1994, we participated in a multi-week-long seminar for leaders at the School of Playback Theatre at Vassar College, New York (founded in 1993), and were among the first graduates. Our joint work was enriched by other previous experience: particularly psychodrama (since 1983 and 1978 respectively) and theatre work (since 1980 and 1976—including student theatre, improvisation, mask work with L. Sheleen, and work with the methods of A. Boal).

Members of the *Spiegelbühne* live for the most part within Frankfurt and its surroundings; a few travel up to eighty kilometers. Ten of our members are German citizens; one is French. We are all "immigrants" to Frankfurt, in the sense that none of us was born and raised in the city or is a native of Frankfurt. Instead six of us come from Hesse, one from Kurpfalz, one from the Rheinland, two from Westphalia, one from upper Frankonia and one from Paris. The sum of the group is representative of a cross-section of the population that has moved to Frankfurt. All of us have lived for various lengths of time at our current residence. However, all have lived for a longer period in stable social contexts, partially alone and/or with a partner and/or child in an apartment or a house. All are or have been married, some remarried. Half of us have at least one child.

All eleven members belong to the middle-class, and work in educational, social or therapeutic professions (adult education, school, university, social work, psychotherapy). With one exception, all of us are involved in psychodrama. At the time of the Symposium at Kassel University in May of 1997, the members were between 36 and 54 years of age (average 45.8). During our time together, themes and stories have arisen from our respective phases of life and existential events in our lives, both professionally and in partnerships. These themes flowed into our rehearsals and performances and included "unemployment," "illness" and/or "death of family members," "loss of parents" and "growing older."

During these four years of unchanged membership, we have experienced good times as well as difficult phases with one another. Together we have tried to find and maintain the balance between private life and group life, rehearsals and performances, continuing training sessions and external supervision, and between individual and ensemble interests.

With our background in psychodrama and sociometry, and experience with group dynamics as well as PT, we had already worked out a certain conceptual framework before establishing the ensemble.

In founding the PT ensemble, we considered the following criteria when talking to specific people or being approached by interested candidates:

Familiarity and/or recommendation. In order to extend a previous basis for relationship, previous acquaintance and/or recommendations from trusted members of the PT movement was required for an interview.

Fellow feeling. Since many private and sometimes intimate themes are touched upon and handled in our work, a mutual compatibility was a necessary basis on which we could easily build the necessary trust for PT work.

Self-experience. In PT work, emotionally deep themes in the players' and audience members' personal stories are often dealt with; and during rehearsals and performances players are often given many and very different roles one after the other. This requires a certain flexibility in taking on roles and sometimes the ability to either appropriately integrate the activated internal processes and reactions, or to postpone these until after the performance. The future members of our group, therefore, should already know their most important personal issues in order to be able to encounter deep emotional processes in themselves and others. In addition, they should be in the position to work constructively within a group since improvising together represents a critical aspect of PT. Individual contributions should fit adequately into the group as a whole, rather than dominate it. In our opinion, to have previous experience in long-term, intensive groups is an important prerequisite for an actor in a stable performance-oriented PT group and enables further development of the required skills. Through our own connections to the psychodrama network, almost all the members of the formed group had similar experience with psychodrama.

Willingness to commit time. From the beginning, the ensemble met once a week for multiple hours of rehearsing. Members were expected to spend an entire evening a week, including travel time, at least from 7 p.m. onwards. This meant taking on this evening appointment to the exclusion of other private and professional activities. Particularly for the freelance workers, this sometimes required reorganizing their schedules.

Willingness to perform in public. An important requirement for joining the ensemble was the willingness to take part in public playback theatre performances—that is, the willingness to risk the adventure of performance in front of an unknown audience, and to trust both the group's and one's own PT skills.

Personal motivation. The interested players' motivation to be involved in playback was, among other things, based on the need to belong to a group, to play and perform, to do something for others and for oneself, and to develop oneself.

These criteria were in part discussed one-on-one, so that the decision to take on a member in all cases was a mutual decision. This decision was always made at first for a 3-month try-out period or until the end of 1993. The decision for each other as members developed during the try-out period was celebrated together in December 1993. Out of this developed the end-of-the-year ritual of having a meal together. Later we had special rituals to welcome new members.

As leaders we set our weekly rehearsals for Thursday, for three hours of training, in the group room of a psychotherapy practice.

The rehearsal room remained the same for about 4 years, and became a sort of home base and an important stabilizing factor for the group. The atmosphere in the rooms was almost private—there was a kitchen, which could be used for the framing activities, such as conversations at the beginning, during breaks, and for celebrations. The group room had a parquet floor and due to its small size a kind of living room atmosphere. Since the first performances took place here, there was an automatic limit to the number of audience members (at most twenty-five to thirty).

In the first few months we [Daniel & Marlies] alternated in the conducting. Since markedly different styles of conducting became apparent, we later conducted for time periods leading up to a coming performance.

From the beginning we pursued the idea that members should increasingly practice and take over the role of conductor. Over time, it became clear that this process required special preparation and a much longer time frame than we had originally presumed.

The group should above all be fun, utilize participants' potentials, and make growth possible, an attitude influenced by our own group-experience, particularly from psychodrama, group dynamics, and theatre work with the Boal method.

Therefore, our concentration lay more in developing individually and as a group and less in the direction of classical forms of theatre.

Performances were an integral part of the group. However, they were not supposed to be an exclusive guideline for the work. Specific preparations were only made at rehearsals directly preceding a performance.

In the back of our minds was the idea of utilizing the connecting function of PT to perform regularly for people in our city and/or in our individual districts—for instance, to support discussions about current developments in the city—thus creating a set place for PT in the public mind.

At first, as leaders, we wanted to handle the possibilities for performances that would be appropriate for our ensemble's stage of development and the PT form of theatre. Later, members should also take on this role and responsibility—for example, by making contacts, preparing contracts, and carrying out other organizational preparations, as well as conducting performances. Every offer and/or self-organized performance would be discussed and decided by the group, as well as scheduled together.

The Early Years

During the first three months—in the simultaneous phases of foundation and try-out period until the end of 1993—it was above all important that everyone could find their own place in the group and work out a sustainable basis for the group as a whole. In the basic training sessions, the individual forms of expression and/or different possibilities for expression became apparent. In regard to the approaching performances, it was necessary to act with one another, and tune the individual acting impulses to fit the situation and the common formation, and under certain circumstances even to withdraw oneself.

By practicing the PT forms, improvising individually as well as together, sharing, and mutual feedback, a good foundation was created over time, a foundation which further developed skills of cooperation between players and the ability to perceive the possibilities for the events on stage.

At this stage, all the members proved somewhat ambivalent about feedback. On the one hand, they wanted to receive clear feedback on the quality of their individual acting, but on the other, they were awkward or shy, uncertain and insecure about this feedback.

In later rehearsals and performances, we would time and again occupy ourselves with the issue of how to find constructive forms of feedback and how to develop these forms and ritualize them.

After the try-out period, a great willingness existed to continue work in the given constellation. Already in these first 12 rehearsals developments could be recognized: increasingly aesthetic and intense scenes were achieved on stage.

However, in the agreement between everyone present, there was no discussion about time frames. At this early date in building the group, there were no thoughts of leaving or being asked to leave—and no one touched on the subject.

Despite the amount of energy required, everyone showed an unusual commitment to the group and to this form of theatre. In the first year, there were rarely absences; everyone was at almost every rehearsal and performance. Certainly, a factor was that each member was well aware of how she spent her free time and had clearly chosen playback theatre.

At the beginning of the try-out period (September 1993), we had already received a preliminary request for a performance at a conference for psychotherapists in February 1994. At the end of the try-out period (December 1993) we discussed this request together and decided to accept it. In addition, we decided to practice beforehand (January 1994) with a performance for family and friends, therefore ensuring a warm reception from our first audience. To celebrate the end of the try-out period and the year, the leaders prepared a meal for the group. A kind of tradition grew out of this event, whereby in the following years both the meal and the celebration would be increasingly created together.

At the beginning of the next year (1994), three performances and a training workshop followed quickly one after another creating an intense period for the group:

January '94: the first performance. The first performance was originally considered a practice run for the February commission. It took place in our rehearsal space in the psychotherapy practice. Each group member could invite one or two audience members out of their private social circle, so that we played before an audience guaranteed to be receptive and could count on open feedback. Therefore, the group had a certain amount of security for their first performance. Altogether, fourteen people attended who were impressed and even enthusiastic about our show. Most would return to our performances time and again.

February '94: the second performance. This performance took place within the context of a psychotherapy conference about "Teaching Psychotherapy." The head of the psychodrama department, who had known us for a long time from psychodrama circles, invited us. The performance took place mid-way through the conference and served as a way for the conference participants to take stock of their issues, impressions, and feelings.

This performance was a challenge for us because the audience was obviously tired and in the mood for easily consumed evening entertainment. At first they were reserved, expressed themselves indirectly, and/or told symbolic stories. Thereafter, attractive and in part uplifting images and scenes developed that were received in an increasingly warm and relaxed atmosphere.

March '94: the third performance. The third performance grew out of a connection to a film director, who had attended the first performance and who had known one of the leaders for years. In the framework of a TV-film project for "Radio Hessen" about various forms of violence among youth, we performed for a group of young female patients from the Frankfurt Center for Eating Disorders. The girls told about their experiences with eating disorders. Due to the technical requirements of filming, the process was occasionally interrupted, but the PT work was, nevertheless, felt to be very intense by all involved, including the film crew.

In the same month (March '94), almost all the members of the *Spiegelbühne* (eight of nine) took part in a training workshop with René Marineau (from Montréal, Canada), which dealt with therapeutic aspects of PT. Parallels became clear on the group level between this training and the second and third performances (which took place in therapeutic contexts). In addition to the everyday topics which had previously dominated, more and more biographical themes arose, which deepened the process and led to closer relationships within the group.

At around this time, external events affected the group. Two members were attacked and robbed while on vacation in Africa; another member of the *Spiegelbühne* became unemployed. Following these events, stories came up during rehearsals about violent threats and dealing with them, and about loss of security and the wish for support and protection.

Shortly thereafter, in May 1994, a workshop with Jonathan Fox was held in which again eight members of the *Spiegelbühne* participated as their second further training. With the title, "Communication and Social Change," the workshop focused on social issues and conflicts, so that this external stimulus refocused our attention on the themes that had arisen in our group.

The impetus gained from such external training courses was an important enrichment for our group work, and since then we have tried to organize training sessions and workshops regularly in Frankfurt for the members of the *Spiegelbühne* and for members of playback outside of our ensemble.

An additional external event became an influential factor in our work that followed. As the only PT performing group in the city at that time, we were asked to be part of a German Christian-Jewish project in the memorial year of 1995 on the theme of "Holocaust and Reconciliation." At first we were interested. But since the project was still in the planning phase and the request to perform was yet unclear, we could not make any definite commitment to participate.

The First Difficulties

Meanwhile, an underlying conflict between two members surfaced. We attempted, at least provisionally, to clarify the issue in an adapted form of PT—the partners in conflict took their seats to the right and left of the conductor and traded off telling how they understood the situation and the aspects of the conflict that they found important. The rest of the group portrayed the stories.

During the rehearsals that followed, additional scenes with taboo themes (aggression, sex, death) were touched upon. These decreased, but would become relevant repeatedly over the next years. In this context, the questions arose: how could we represent these taboo subjects adequately on stage, and how could a misrepresentation be avoided?

During this time, in which we were occupied with many difficult situations and group issues, no performances were held. We needed time and space for the internal processes and individual themes. We felt that additional themes surrounding a performance might exceed the group's and leaders' capacities. In addition, the difficult group situation might influence the performance like a warped mirror.

Later, after a certain consolidation within the group, the preparation and concentration required by a performance would become a mutual task and aid in overcoming the difficulties. Thereafter, the performances took place on rehearsal days so that no additional time was required from the members. At these performances, the influence of the group room on the show became increasingly apparent, both on the behavior of the audience and on the themes of the stories.

A distinction developed, therefore, between the performances in the group room for a smaller number of invited guests out of familiar circles and potential clients, and other opened or closed performances in other environments for an often unknown public.

At the end of the first year, after thirty-three training sessions, which were attended by almost all members, we had achieved a certain level of cohesion in the group.

Following the first consolidation phase, signs of the phase known in group dynamics as "differentiation" appeared during the second year. Beyond this, after the summer break, a certain "normalization" period set in—members continued to be highly committed. However time after time individuals were absent, in other words parallel to the difficult group situation, the regularity of rehearsal attendance dropped.

During the first half of the second year, tensions increased. At first this was caused by the leaders' enthusiasm to introduce ideas from their training program at the School of PT during the vacation, which caused uncertainty and reluctance among the group members. After such a long summer break, they wanted and needed to start with basic regrouping, instead of immediately dealing with new forms—an important point for us as leaders and members.

In addition, the project for the Holocaust Memorial Year cast a shadow over us. The group tried to approach this difficult subject slowly. During preparatory rehearsals, a teller became upset by a distorted enactment.

Feelings of collective guilt and shame arose among the German Christian members, accentuated by the fact that one of the leaders is of Jewish heritage. Parallel to this, the number of absences from rehearsals increased—in retrospect, one can see that this was a sign that the subject was beyond our ensemble's capacities in the present situation. We had to conclude that both the leaders and group members needed much more time to approach and prepare for this difficult theme than was possible before the project began.

At the fourth performance in the group room, shortly before Christmas 1994, the focus was on taboos, painful experiences, and being torn inside. During this performance a difficult situation arose. After a scene about visiting a dead relative's grave, the teller reacted with an unmistakable "No!" and a clear rejection of the representation.

This first strong "No!" was not easy to process and produced an intense discussion in the group, during which a number of questions arose. How can the ensemble best do justice to the story and avoid upsetting the teller? How can a workable atmosphere be created, in which a storyteller feels comfortable to expose all feelings, as well as negative ones, about a scene? How can the group and each individual accept and integrate such a possible rejection during and after the performance?

A third training workshop with Jonathan Fox in May 1995 on "Metaphors in PT" offered a sort of answer to the question about how such difficult subjects could be appropriately represented. Thereafter, we distanced ourselves from participation in the Holocaust Memorial Year project. We concluded that we could not do justice to the project in the time available. A deep involvement with this subject only seemed possible with a slower, more careful preparation over a longer period. Beyond this, the risks were too great for our still young PT group. The topic was dropped for a while, and rehearsal attendance rose again.

We also determined that in the case of a longer absence, only those players should perform who had at least attended the last rehearsal before the planned performance.

At an additional one-day supervision led by Jonathan Fox for all the *Spiegelbühne* members, we experimented among other things with the idea of fully utilizing the relatively crowded group room space by alternating players during the performance between the stage and audience, so that only a part of the players were on stage at one time.

Later, we developed the role of the observing actor, who sits in the audience during the entire performance in order to comment and give feedback from this perspective after the performance.

Also the aspect of conducting took up much time, since among the leaders there were increasing tensions and conflicts. In part, this was certainly due to mixed roles (ie. private couple and leading couple), and to the unreconciled competition between different styles of conducting. However, it was also an indication of being drained and overburdened, since we were constantly aware of how much of our time was taken up in preparation before and after sessions, in light of the many aspects of such a PT group—such as, the processing and confrontations in addition to the actual training and performing time. In retrospect, due to our initial burst of energy and enthusiasm for PT, we underestimated the time commitment required of us and should have freed more space from our time-consuming professions. For this reason, this phase was very difficult for us as leaders. The necessity to create more time, by delegating roles and responsibilities between the members of the group, became more and more urgent. At the supervision, we examined the possibility that the group had to give feedback and support to the leaders.

"Time" was therefore the apt title of our next performance: we accompanied a speech about time in the context of the annual conference of the DFP (The German Psychodramatists' Association) [*Deutscher Fachverband für Psychodrama*]. This was an experiment in which we diverged from the classical form of a performance: during the speech, following particular sections, we converted the audience's feedback into scenes. With this performance, we introduced a large number of our psychodrama colleagues to PT work.

Expansion

In the second year, besides differentiation and recognizing limitations there was much expansion: in the repertoire of themes, in the rehearsal space, in the number of offers, and the number of players.

For the first time, we moved a rehearsal into the private sphere. We rehearsed at the home of two of our members (their house warming), and for the first time a member conducted the rehearsal.

Following the performance in December 1994 in the group room, two audience members voiced their interest in joining the ensemble. Therefore, at the beginning of the new year (1995), or in the middle of *Spiegelbühne*'s second year, these two became members after a try-out period of four rehearsals, a group discussion, and a ritual. Both are musicians, so that the until then mostly sung music could now be augmented by musical instruments. The element of music grew to be a vital part of rehearsals and performances.

The group's consolidation became apparent at the next performance in the group room. The invited audience included more and more family members and colleagues from work. Our members' families, who also had to carry the burden of their interest in PT and tolerate the time-consuming commitment, took greater interest. They attended performances more and more often, a trend which would continue.

In the second year of performing, we also received more requests to perform for larger audiences on larger stages. Therefore, it became urgent to find a larger rehearsal space (in which we had more possibilities for practicing larger movements, in order to learn how to fill a large stage).

In preparation for a performance with a large audience in the autumn, we had the opportunity to gain experience with a larger stage and a large public performance shortly before the summer break. We were offered the use of a room at the University of Frankfurt, and the chance to perform for the first time in public without knowing who would attend. Unfortunately, it hadn't been possible for us to practice in advance in this space and to make it our own. An additional difficulty was the extreme heat in this room, with its defective air-conditioning.

Shortly before the performance, a tense atmosphere developed, our group was a little frayed and nervous. The audience was very heterogeneous and much larger than we had been used to in the group room (about sixty). With certainty, this performance was one of our less successful. However, we learned much, and it had an interesting effect, namely, the audience's stories reflected the performers' group process. For instance, one story was about a chaotic wedding in the desert.

This second phase, up until the seventieth training session, can be characterized as a phase between certainty and uncertainty, familiarity and novelty, increasing internal differentiation and aiming for expansion, as well as a phase in which we improved our understanding of time management, space needs, and personal limitations.

Following the summer break, the initial rehearsals of the third year were characterized by preparations for a performance at a big convention. During the preparations for this performance, a crisis developed due to multiple problems, some on our side and some on the side of the organizer.

On our side, due to timing we could hardly meet all together for a rehearsal. In addition, the planned conductor was forced, due to family matters, to travel for an extended time until shortly before the performance. The other leader was increasingly tied up with the preparations and the prospect of leading the convention and therefore was not in the position to support the group in this situation.

On the part of the organization, in the printing of the program for the convention there was a notable omission. Our performance failed to appear in it. Evidently, the organizer had "forgotten" to leave time and room for us. Also in a poster printed later to announce the evening festivities, PT was written into the lowest margin and with a different time than the one we had verbally agreed to—now the performance would take place later in the evening, in the middle of the festivities instead of at the beginning. In the discussion with the organizer it was clear that the original agreement to the conditions of performing had been changed without consulting us, and therefore the necessary framework (time, space, attention) could no longer be created in the short time left.

Since we could not develop any alternative with the organizer, we made the decision, after rehearsing in the space, not to perform under these changed conditions. Thus, at the last minute we cancelled the performance.

Under given circumstances it seemed more important to us, on the one hand, not to expose the ensemble in their present state to such difficult performing conditions, and on the other, to prevent our PT work from degenerating at the same time into "buffet entertainment."

One member of our group was, nevertheless, registered as a participant at the convention, and as the only "representative" of the group became a target for the organizer's anger and for that of some of the convention visitors. Thereafter the themes "being abandoned," "blame" and "being in trouble" played a large role in the group.

We determined that we needed to plan our performances even more carefully, securing enough space, time, and attention, in order for the PT work to exhibit its power.

At the eighth performance in the group room in December 1995 the stories circled around themes such as "mixed messages," "separation," and the "consequences thereof."

Following the cancellation of the big performance in the autumn, we, as leaders, had reached a turning-point, and decided together to take part in leader supervision with a supervisor and psychoanalyst in Frankfurt (13 sessions from November 1995 to July 1996). The subjects of the supervision sessions included the sociometry of the group and its sociodynamic deep structure, the positions of the leaders in the group, the dynamic among couples (ourselves and the other couple), the different styles of leadership, handling tension and conflicts, and the connection to our own biographical themes.

Over the next year, the members took on even more tasks and responsibilities, first through their initiative and efforts connected with the development of publicity materials (designing a logo, information-sheet, and an ensemble T-shirt), then increasing efforts towards opportunities to perform.

We continued to pursue the goal of integrating participants into the role of conductor for rehearsals and performances in order to increase the repertoire of roles and to expand the possibilities for performance and thus raise the quality of our presentation. It became clear through the current group concept and the format of training that we had partially achieved the difficult transition to a rotating leadership. Such a fundamental change in the framework required time and preparation in small steps in order to be accepted by everyone, since such a transformation of the group concept could cause a crisis and threaten the group's cohesion. The verbal consent had to be converted into action in appropriate phases.

In addition, the subject of competition among members and towards the leaders had made us aware of other things.

As a next step, the invited guests at the ninth performance were personally greeted and received by the hosting players. At the tenth performance, we then experimented with two group members in the audience for the entire performance, rather than substituting players part way through, in order to get more qualified feedback for our acting from the audience's perspective.

We also experimented with various forms of audience warm-ups, including movement, which proved less successful and was given up thereafter.

Following the next training session in May 1996 with Jonathan Fox on the topic "Aesthetics in PT" (at which six *Spiegelbühne* members participated) we strengthened our use of cloth and focused on our aesthetics in the portrayal of scenes.

During the Easter vacation of 1996, one member of the group took part in a conducting workshop with Jonathan Fox, and shortly thereafter the entire group had an internal training session with Jo Salas on strengthening the integration of music into our work. Music had gained in importance, and the role of the musician had become increasingly meaningful. It was possible to view competition as an opportunity to discover and build resources.

Following this, almost the entire group took part in the first German-speaking PT conference in Bad Bevensen, which three *Spiegelbühne* members had helped organize. Thereafter, a *Spiegelbühne* member again led a rehearsal for the group.

At the final performance of the season, we played for the first time privately for a member, at a garden party, and also for the first time outdoors. In preparation, we rehearsed in a meadow along the Main River, in front of a cloth backdrop, which we hung between two trees. This theatre space, surrounded by trees in open nature, meant very difficult acoustics and much distraction from the events of the surroundings. It thus presented a challenge to the players' concentration and the carrying of voices.

The third year ended after the 107th training session.

Now an advanced phase began. The pressure to perform well was met by our own standards, although it would arise again in times of crisis. By now we had gotten to know the boundaries that members had set for themselves. We respected them, or developed a peaceful coexistence with them, and regulated the closeness and distance to one another. PT was experienced as an important resource by all of us.

That autumn was an intense time for the group. Many events—sickness, saying goodbye and new beginnings, loss and mourning in families—were coped with, in addition to which the leaders were handling unusually heavy workloads and therefore lacked time.

Again and again, we debated about space and time and chose to only accept those offers which fulfilled our interests, and to be less guided by our desire to perform. As always, payment did not play a role, we only expected the costs to be covered. With the offers that were accepted under this consideration, we were willing to go to great lengths. The themes often reflected our inner group process.

At the immediate beginning of our fourth year, we performed once again in our private sphere—at the wedding of one of our members. As an exception, we had decided to show only a few pairs and fluid sculptures as short entertainment upon presenting our joint gift. Since we could choose the time and framework and could enjoy ourselves as guests the rest of the time at the celebration, it was a fine start for the playback season which followed.

Performance Challenges

The first commissioned performance of the season, for the jubilee of a large therapy institute in Würzburg, highlighted the following themes: "consolidating an identity," "reflecting on the past," and "developing new perspectives."

As a consequence of our past experience, we took considerable time to thoroughly prepare for this performance and, for example, rehearsed in large spaces. Also the contact with the organizer beforehand, the preparation of the room in which we would perform, and creating optimal conditions was very time-consuming. In keeping with this, the atmosphere in the group was very supportive. For the first time after a long period, the group was fully assembled on stage. For the first time ever, partners were present—six couples.

For this big performance, we played for an audience of about 200. We performed in a large room, which we had been able to set up to suit us. We worked for the first time with stage lights, and the musician sat on a platform at players' and audience members' eye-level. The partners participated as "roadies." For example, they took care of contact with the organizer during the warm up, prevented disturbances, and in part looked after the lighting.

To begin with, the conference participants were heavily influenced by the situation that immediately preceded us. The keynote-speaker had died a few days before, and a mourning colleague delivered his speech.

The playback work offered an important opportunity to relieve the strain, which the participants intensely utilized. The difficult situation became increasingly relaxed and the different generations in the institution found room to tell their stories.

They spoke about looking back at the beginnings, crises, possible prospects for the institute, and opportunities for the future in an increasingly difficult employment landscape. It was clear that playback theatre was helpful as a means to cope.

At our next performance, which again took place in the group room, three generations appeared in all the stories, and in the following performance shortly before Christmas, for the first time a woman far advanced in pregnancy sat in the audience. Reflecting societal developments, one teller talked about the threat of unemployment, which would in the following year also become acute in our group.

At the celebration of the year's end, which we planned together, each brought something to contribute that they had prepared at home, and added it to the composition prepared by all. Even in the shaping of the celebration, changes were apparent in the increasingly differentiated roles and members taking on various responsibilities.

Influenced by the events in our families at the beginning of the new year, an intense sharing took place in the group about death and the loss of family members. In this mutual exchange of our existential experiences a closeness and openness grew among us.

The next performance was completely influenced by this and the images and stories portrayed were particularly intense and exact.

At the following sixteenth performance, we let ourselves be tempted into changing the planned framework. Due to an unusually high demand we quickly moved the performance location from the group room to a room at the university, with which we were already familiar.

The audience consisted of a number of individuals, some smaller groups and one larger group. This larger subgroup had journeyed there together and was therefore already well warmed up to one another. Therefore, it was difficult to bring the various groups together.

The stories told included those of "threat," "limitations," "being attacked," and "defending."

At the following large performance at a memorial conference in honor of Karlfried Graf Dürckheim, an important theme became the discomfort following the loss of a spiritual leader and feeling uncertain about the path of spiritual searching. Although three of our members were unable to attend, the others participated in the conference. In the group, a general feeling of alienation arose in the context of the conference events, and the irritation and stress grew due to high expectations. By withdrawing into a separate room and intensely discussing and processing the obvious effects of the general atmosphere on the members of the ensemble, we were able to regain cohesion. It was again possible to concentrate on the situation's demands, the audience's needs, and our opportunity. The scenes of the performance dealt with "the necessity to break taboos," "the dangers of doing so," "the fear of being alone, and "being responsible for one's own path."

At this conference, it became particularly clear that PT is well suited for the closing ceremony of a conference when it is well prepared. We also learned how important it is that the performers are able to find the appropriate distance from and/or closeness to the audience. Through this experience, the spiritual themes resonating in our group became tangible.

In April 1997, five members of the *Spiegelbühne* took part in the next training session with Jonathan Fox on "The Themes that Connect the Stories in PT," and at about the same time, the musician attended the workshop offered in another region by Jo Salas about music in PT.

In preparation for a necessary change of rehearsal space, due to the future unavailability of the group room we had used until then, we transferred our rehearsals to a new room which was three times the size of our previous space.

The atmosphere in this new room was more impersonal than before, and the switch and the pending loss of the group room as a set rehearsal space and home base for the group posed a decisive point. After the initial discomfort and diffusion, the group slowly adjusted to the new space and prepared for the next performance.

For the first time, this performance was organized by a member of the group, who was also responsible for building the contact and for the preparations on location. It would take place in Thuringia at the annual meeting of a denominational umbrella organization of family-, marriage-, and life counseling centers on the subject of relationships ("Him, Her, and the Third in the Relationship"). During the preparations, we dealt with the differences between East and West Germany after the reunification and continued to work with the spiritual themes. We considered prejudices concerning the Christian Church from our own backgrounds, memories, and religious upbringings. Only one member participated in the conference and served as a bridge between us and the events of the day.

For the first time, we traveled as a group into East Germany to perform before an audience of about 200. We arrived in small groups the night before and rehearsed briefly before we joined the conference festivities at around 9 p.m. The next morning, Sunday, we were supposed to perform after breakfast and before the closing church service, in order for the participants to evaluate the conference together.

A platform had been set up as a stage in the large room and due to the poor acoustics, a microphone had to be used. Since we began preparing ourselves early (7 a.m.), it was possible to interact with the East German custodians, who had arranged the room and chairs to serve our needs. For them we played a few pairs and fluids on the existing social differences and their reactions to these.

The audience, which included a few members of the clergy, were well warmed up after three days of working together. Some very deep stories were told, dealing with the tensions and conflicts in the supporting organizations regarding spiritual experiences, religion, sexuality, and taboos.

At this last performance preceding the Symposium in Kassel, we made use of the supportive atmosphere to completely substitute the players with audience members for the first time, an experience which participants valued and enjoyed. In the original sense of PT, it was possible for people to take their stories into their own hands and to perform for themselves.

German-Speaking PT Network

Parallel to building up *Spiegelbühne*, it was important to us as leaders to maintain contact with other playback theatre groups and to actively help create a German-speaking PT network. In the autumn of 1994 the first meeting of those interested in German-speaking playback took place in Stuttgart. This initiative, from Annette Henne, Jürgen Hermann and Marlies Arping, was a result of the completed Practice and Leadership classes at the School of Playback Theatre in New York, also attended by Marianne Tobler, Daniel Feldhendler and Susanne Ramsauer. Around 25 participants adopted the idea of continual communication through such regular meetings.

As a result, in the autumn of 1995 the second meeting took place in Offenbach. There it was decided to organize a large conference at which as many as possible active playbackers and people interested in playback could get to know one another and exchange information in order to build up a network for the German-speaking countries.

Three members of the *Spiegelbühne* belonged to this organizing committee.

In April 1996, about ninety people participated in the first large conference in Bad Bevensen (in Lower Saxony), with Jo Salas and Jonathan Fox as guests. At that time the idea of a first PT Symposium at the University of Kassel was already being discussed. Themes emerged for discussion, including subliminal competition between existing groups, differences in styles and concepts between the generations of active playbackers, and sharing among playback theatre leaders (as in the form of intervision already practiced at the PT meeting in December 1996 in Zurich).

Conclusion and Perspectives

The ensemble is relatively homogeneous in regard to age and social backgrounds.

The four-year process of development of our playback theatre group can be divided into the following phases: intense group dynamics, first consolidation and preliminary integration; oscillation between security and insecurity, limitation and expansion; consolidation of our identity and securing the quality of our dramatic expression; and wider external orientation.

In our work together, subjects came up which formed a running theme touching on the fundamental human issues of birth and death and sickness and health, in our own generation (partners, siblings, friends, and colleagues), the preceding (parents') generation, and the following generation of children (our own or those of our sisters and brothers). Other themes dealt with partnerships (everyday life, marriage, divorce, crises, family planning) and careers (everyday life, changes, dealing with conflicts and tensions, coping with crises and unemployment).

A trend arose towards a stronger external orientation, also recognizable in our choice of space. To begin with, rehearsals and performances took place only in the group room and/or partially in our members' private sphere, which encouraged introspection (group building and internal understanding). Later, we chose other spaces for practicing and performing and so opened ourselves for other audiences, other issues, and a larger public.

In addition to the continuous interaction between individual, political and spiritual themes of the group, the future life of *Spiegelbühne* will probably be greatly influenced by the following: the change of location and the consequences this will have on our group cohesion; the increased incorporation of members into the role of conductors and their individual further training in PT; and possible changes in the composition of the group due to changing priorities of individual members and/or personal and career changes.

We have described the process of our group from an internal perspective, since as involved participants we are affected on many levels. Influenced by the inner life of the group, on the one hand, and by our relationship as a married couple, who founded and lead the group, on the other, we can only be aware of parts of the entire process.

Supervision and support in our roles as leaders was important to us through discourse with other experienced leaders, being embedded in an international PT context, and aiding the formation of a German-speaking PT movement.

And naturally, despite all the self-awareness and the knowledge of our own limitations and group dynamics, there still remain blind spots, false perceptions, temptations, entanglements, fears, rivalries, aggression, and spent capacities.

We attempt, through continued communication and reflection, to stay on track. For us this often involves recognizing, accepting, and overcoming the differences between our ideals and realistic possibilities with humor and good will.

In the end, the challenge lies in growing together and gaining awareness of people and the stories they tell.

Note

[1] Translated from German by Rachel Getzoff, in cooperation with the authors.

Playback Portrait

ROBERT SCHERBACH & ASHA RICHARD
Germany

What's your professional education? Tell us about yourselves.

Asha: Our professional background is quite diverse. I was born in 1962 and went to acting school in Vienna after completing my carpentry training. Besides acting I earned a degree in psychology, studying in Berlin and later Frankfurt.

Robert: I was born in '58, studied social work, drove a taxi for a few years, trained as a clown, and then did street theatre. In addition, we have trained as psychodramatists, NLP master practitioners, massage therapists, and taken numerous workshops and courses, for example with Augusto Boal and with Jonathan Fox, whose School of Playback Theatre we graduated from last year.

How did you discover PT?

A: After I saw a performance of Annette Henne's playback theatre group in 1991, I was fascinated with this theatre form... and with Annette's heartfelt manner.

R: Asha told me about it, I liked the idea, and the two of us went to Schaffhausen to a playback workshop with Annette. We both caught the playback bug. That was the beginning.

What are you doing with PT at the moment?

A: We're working with group impulses that arise spontaneously during the action. We deliver a kind of meta-idea for a few seconds, then reintegrate into the regular action. It's like a picture behind the picture.

R: For next year we're planning public performances in the

113

community with our adult theatre company, as well as an ongoing project at a juvenile detention center. We'll also have our five-year anniversary.

A: In addition to our annual training weekend and our special one-day training with a particular teacher (for example, martial arts), we have hired a singing teacher for 1999, who will work with us every six weeks, both individually and as a chorus.

R: For a year we have had a children's company. The children's playback theatre group became "The Play-Theatre, by children who went out to enact stories." The children develop their own rules for group dynamics and we create new forms of improvisational acting. One new form we worked out for this group, for example, is "der Fächer" (the fan). The actors go out one after the other and take several levels on the stage, so that the picture you get is the impression of a "Fächer." It is more structured than a fluid sculpture in order to manage the spontaneity of the group (each one frequently wants to be the first).

A: And we're planning a day-long playback theatre event for the German-speaking playback community, for us to come together, without too much organizational effort, and tell each other stories and play them back for each other, and so on... all day long.

You are a married couple who co-lead playback theatre. What's it like?

R: We're a couple and working like this is excellent for us. Living and working together was a choice from the very beginning.

A: In all other areas of our theatre work we also lead as a team, in this way the group or audience has twice the scope to relate to the leader. Furthermore one doesn't face leadership decisions all alone. We can check on and enrich each other.

You've just had a baby. How has Noah changed your playback life?

R: Of course our lives have changed through our child, and as self-employed theatre professionals, we have the possibility to bring work and life together.

A: In the end it's a question of organization, of the social environment and the support you get, as well as the amount of other work, which we keep relatively small.

You're part of the "free theatre," unattached to a major institution. From your perspective, do you think that PT has a future as a theatre form in Germany?

R: We've been doing Freies Theater for six years. Our company, DAZU Theater, pursues the idea of the "absichtlichen Zufalls," coincidence happening on purpose. We create a formal and precise frame in which the spontaneous can develop. For us theatre is always a place of gathering and encounter as well as of the unforeseen. So there is a balance between enjoyment and challenge.

A: Risk-free and easily digestible theatre doesn't interest us. A non-commercial and risk-taking independent theatre, which values community and honors the possibility of the unforeseen encounter/connection is as rare as a needle in a haystack... but it does exist!

R: For us as free theatre people playback is a timely idea, as long as it doesn't slip into mere amusement, the number of spectators are kept small, and the artistry is visible alongside the social expertise... And there are further criteria...

A: And even when all the criteria are fulfilled, there is still the question whether it is artistic theatre, which is not the same as good theatre. In any case it certainly is good theatre.

A RITUAL FOR OUR TIME

Jonathan Fox

Every playback theatre actor is familiar with the disconcerting experience that often comes just when a performance is over. An audience member will come up, shake your hand warmly as if in congratulation, and say: "But tell me. What is the purpose of it anyway?"

We groan inwardly, because to answer such a philosophical question when we are still vibrating from the last teller's story is pretty tough. Unfortunately, even in calm moments, far away from the stage lights and applause, it's not much easier.

For in fact the playback process is not simple to describe or understand. One reason is its flexibility: it can be adapted to many different specific needs in education and mental health as well as function as artistic theatre. This means that as a method it spans the conventional categories of theatre, psychology, and education.

Nevertheless, the question is valid: What *is* the purpose of playback theatre?

In this essay, I will attempt to frame an answer. I will discuss the theme first from the point of view of the community—that is, the groups which experience playback theatre, either in ticketed performances or a special setting (such as school, workplace, or community center). Then I will turn to the playback performers themselves and some of the challenges they face in fulfilling the promise of their form.

Red Threads

I'd like to begin with some stories.

The teller, a woman in her twenties, tells about being on a trek in Asia and getting lost. She and her friend were far from a village. Darkness was falling, and no one came to help. The setting was strange and scary. There was nothing to do but camp out in a kind of shepherd's hut. The teller felt miserable at their bad luck. But nothing bad happened. In fact, they woke up to find themselves in an incredibly beautiful spot, surrounded by rhodo-dendrons, with snow-capped mountains in the distance. Terror had turned into joy; threat into blessing.

The story that followed right after took place in New York City.

A middle-aged woman tells about meeting the daughter of an acquain-tance of her mother's, a woman from overseas—a country in Asia, to be exact. The teller (who used to live in New York, but had moved away) had expected to have to show the visitor around. She feared it would be a troublesome and perhaps boring afternoon. As it turned out, the young woman was not only kind and interesting, but also very knowledgeable about the city. In fact, as the day progressed the teller realized that the young woman was showing her around. Instead of being the leader, she was being led; instead of the giver, she was being given to. It was a pleas-ant surprise.

Let me point out some features of this storytelling process. These two stories form a kind of point and counterpoint for each other. While they both share a theme of unexpected happiness, in the first there is no guide, or bringer of joy, while in the second there is such a figure in the presence of the young woman. The counterpoint creates a kind of dialogue. It is as if in the first story the teller is saying, "Sometimes we are lost and alone, and it turns out all right." And the second teller answers, "That may be true, yes. And it is also true that sometimes, even when we are *not* lost and alone, we can have a surprise and find ourselves guided by a stranger, finding new pleasure in old territory."

It is important to remind ourselves here that in this example the pro-cess of the tellers coming forward was spontaneous; the conductor did not invite one kind of story or another. Yet even though each teller told her own personal tale, the stories connected on a social level. This "red thread" can be understood as containing a kind of folk wisdom.

Another feature of this process is that inevitably, there is not one thread, but many. For instance, the first teller has an epiphany in a remote spot in Asia; while in the second story, Asia, in the form of the young immigrant, comes to the West ("You don't have to go to the other side of the world"). In the first story, joy follows fear, disappointment, and despair, while in the second, there is nothing so dramatic ("Even a boring obligation can turn into something unexpectedly wonderful.") In the first story, the teller is a young adult, while in the second story, the teller is old enough to be the mother of the first, ("Adventure is for youth, to be sure, but even when you are my age, such joy can still be found"). In playback these "messages" are communicated through the medium of enacted story, through movement, color, music, and metaphoric action.

A third feature derives from the context. We have learned that the story elements, in addition to speaking to the community in a general way, usually relate very specifically to the circumstances of the group. In this case, the audience comprised students at the start of a long training workshop. It is natural at such a time for students to be fearful of getting overwhelmed and "lost." Others often worry that the course might be dull and unchallenging. In this case, the course was a PT training, and both tellers, each in her way, seemed to be reminding their peers to trust in the spontaneity process.

The way the red threads carry through a playback event is so rich that as conductor I like to let the process be as undirected as possible, worried that if I make too many suggestions, I will in fact restrict this often unconscious form of dialogue (there are special cases where I act otherwise—see section below on Shamanic Conducting).

Now let me go to a second event, which took place during a playback theatre workshop in the USA on Social Change. There were twelve participants, ten whites and two African-Americans. During the first two days the stories were about white children experiencing the reality of living in a racially divided land.

In one, the teller at age five witnesses prejudice for the first time as she sees her aunt speak insultingly to a beloved servant. In another, the teller tells about being a teenager as the family moves to the suburbs to get away from the blacks.

Following these stories, with the encouragement of the leader, one of the African-Americans tells. It is a story about his grandfather, in whose house he had grown up—in particular, his grandfather's personal dignity and high standards for his family. There is a strong incident of racism in the story, in the form of grave injustice suffered by the grandfather at work. But there is a stronger theme of overcoming racism. In fact, the teller never knows what his grandfather suffers until much later, when he learns about it as an adult, because the grandfather had kept it from the children.

In the unfolding of the stories in this workshop, the same contrapuntal elements are present. What stands out here is that with the story of the black teller, we hear from the "other voice." One of the strongest features of playback theatre is that it allows diverse voices to be heard in a context of empathy.

A final point: the stories told by the whites were not heroic tales, nor were they victim stories. Instead they were accounts involving shameful deeds of their own families, painful to share and to watch. Such honesty enables a confrontation with truth that is all too rare in a human society where countries and their institutions often demand heroic official histories. Playback theatre honors the people's voice, be it joyful or ashamed, triumphant or oppressed. One of its purposes is to let this voice be heard, before witnesses, in all its richness and variety.

Restoring Oral Traditions

What we have seen so far in these examples is the presence of a special kind of discussion taking place through the tellers' stories. It is not an ordinary discussion, because it occurs through scenes enacted on a stage. We find more action and fewer words than in ordinary discussion. Moreover, the emphasis is not cognitive. Ideas may be inherent in the stories; we may be able to read a message or moral in them. Often insight will follow the enactment. But ultimately, the playback stories are *stories*, with setting, character, plot, and image. And as in stories, the value, or meaning, often reveals itself only indirectly. For example, in the stories described above, there are points being made not only about racism and prejudice in America, but about adults' behavior to children and the place of human dignity.

These aspects bring us back in touch with the oral tradition, which is rooted in sensory perception and welcomes emotion. The modern professional world has tended to champion other values. Playback has often been looked upon suspiciously by institutions, because it appears "soft," and does not focus directly on problems or return concrete solutions. Actually, today, more than two decades after playback first started, there is a more receptive climate to playback's holistic kind of communication because scholars have been reframing the argument. Sensory interaction with the environment, iconic thinking, need for narrative, and the marriage of feeling and thought are fundamental, it is now believed, to the human mind.[1] Thus playback now can be appreciated for the fullness of its approach to communication, which will often provide the *conditions* necessary to find a truly enduring answer.

Since playback theatre engages many aspects of our intelligence, it penetrates our consciousness in a particularly profound manner. Amazingly, we remember the stories we see in playback theatre. I remember the first story I ever conducted, almost thirty years ago. The teller is a person I see only once in ten years, but the truth contained in her story, which was about getting lost and finding her way, has also remained with me and acts as a kind of ever-present guide as I go about my life.

The concept of discourse implies exchange between equals, and there is an implied belief in playback theatre that if we can speak and listen to each other in this deep way, good will come of it. In a playback performance, we are *all* experts, in that we all have stories with potential answers embodied within them—this holds for the youngest child, the humblest adult, the most wizened elder. The task of the playback leader or team is to create the atmosphere in which the folk feel free to come forth and tell.

Those of us who have been telling, acting out, and witnessing playback stories over a long time know the value of this communal telling. It is one of the reasons, I believe, why there tends to be so little turnover in playback theatre performing companies: the process is life-enhancing on such a deep level that we want to stay involved.

To sum up what we have concluded so far, playback theatre offers a kind of community conversation through stories, and this conversation, even though it contains not one, but many themes, and is often indirect in making its points, gives scope for the expression of a popular truth.

Awake to the World

Not always, but often enough that we recognize it as normal, the audience feels *good* after playback theatre. Of course, this is true of most theatre as entertainment. But in this case, the feeling is deeper, since the subject of the play is the audience themselves, their life-world. The process of identifying one's own story and witnessing another's often leads to a feeling of communal renewal.

This renewal takes place on a number of levels. The first is individual. I can best illustrate it by noting the changes in a teller's body tension during the enactment of his story. At the start, he will be more or less tense. He may still be searching for the precise thing to tell. He may not quite trust the conductor sitting next to him, asking questions. He may feel shy of the others watching. Once the enactment begins, the body tenses in another way. There is excitement and intense engagement now, as he watches the actors take on the challenge of portraying his life. Then, when the actors hit a chord of truth, capturing the essence of what he was trying, so imperfectly and incompletely, to convey, there is a sudden relaxation, often accompanied by a sigh. Then there is a final body shift, once the enactment is completed, and the teller can take in the empathic response of the audience. The teller returns to his chair in a very different state than when he left it. He is likely to be smiling (sometimes through lingering tears). It is not easy to describe this new state-of-being: He is "in touch." He feels "lighter."

The second level is social. The playback experience reduces the sense of alienation often felt by the inhabitants of the modern community. Of course, playback now exists in a variety of places, from large cities to small towns, and in many different cultures. But despite this variety, it can be generally said that more often than not in a public setting the audience comes as strangers to one another. Thus there is always a tension in the audience as well as among prospective tellers, since there is no way of knowing what the play will be about or how it will be handled. Members of the audience are naturally wary. This wariness will be present even among a group that is already established, such as a school class or a group of fellow workers. The social interaction that is such an important part of the playback experience works to dispel the fear of being among strangers, planting in its stead a sense of connectedness. Audience members often are amazed that they are able to participate in a personal and meaningful experience with people who only hours ago felt so distant. Their aloofness is transmuted into a correspondingly strong openness to discourse, and even afterwards, as they exchange comments, often a joyful feeling.[2]

Finally, the very sensuousness of live theatre, with its sights and sounds, images and rhythms, helps bring us out of our shell and open us up to the physical world around us. For those of us living in cities and caught up in cerebral matters, the playback experience constitutes a wake-up for our senses.

Taking into consideration these mood effects on the individual, social, and environmental level, we can say that overall, playback theatre focuses the individual and group energy in such a way that the audience undergoes a trance experience, often feeling both energized and relaxed afterwards, along with a sense of physical and psychological renewal. We come away from the performance awake and open to the world. This effect is not unlike what people have experienced since time immemorial after special communal ceremonies. After playback theatre we can hear once more the leaves making music in the trees; see again the sunlight dancing on the water; enjoy pleasurable and supportive contact with others; find new hope.[3]

On the Threshold of the New

One can easily imagine other kinds of discourse-enhancing activities, such as a public debate, classroom discussion, or even a therapy session. And one can easily bring to mind other kinds of relaxing, enlivening experience, such as a yoga class, ballroom dancing, or a walk in the forest. What is not so common, perhaps, is an experience that accomplishes both. What makes this possible in playback is its nature as a heightened dramatic event.

By comparison, we might think of a wedding or a funeral in our times. Or communal dances in other times that had the purpose of preparing hunters for the hunt, or healers to lay hands on the sick. These kinds of rituals are utterly serious and intended to produce transformation.[4]

It is commonplace to say that our modern age has seen a decline in ritual, such that many people today hardly know its power. Thus playback theatre is often asked to perform a more limited task, such as to teach shy adolescents expressiveness, or company managers team-building techniques. And it can accomplish these objectives, but in my view only in the framework of the more profound goal associated with a ritual.

The playback theatre event frequently begins with flatness. The audience, unfamiliar with the form and its ritual process, waits suspiciously. But slowly, as the ritual unfolds and people get caught up in it, feelings rise, with the inevitable consequence that a fully undertaken playback event will be strongly emotional. The music will play a haunting refrain. The actors will render a scene with particular power. The conductor will use just the right word at the right time. And suddenly a teller will spring out of her chair, to tell a story that comes from a buried corner of her soul. And this story will spring another teller into a deep nexus of feeling and memory. This letting loose of emotional energy is a natural part of the ritual.

Sometimes the informality of the playback theatre stage, in which actors are present as themselves, often relating to the audience between stories in a human way, is deceptive. Moreover, playback can take place anywhere, in rooms belonging to everyday life, with virtually no equipment. But there is nothing informal about the ritual.

Not long ago in Israel, I conducted a demonstration of playback in a university classroom for community workers. The conditions were not stable—people came and went; there was little sense of decorum in the crowded classroom space. Nevertheless, I proceeded. Space was cleared for a stage; at its rear was put a row of chairs for audience actors. To the right of the stage I placed two chairs, for myself as conductor and the teller, who would come from the group. In short, the ritual space was set. In my manner, I tried to give a sense of the temporal aspect of ritual as well: at a certain point, my words became more formal, their pace slow and rhythmic.

The first teller told an everyday tale of waking up in the morning. Volunteers from the audience acted it out. Then a second teller came forward and told a life-threatening secret of twenty years. The secret was that he had been a political radical in another country and had committed violent, illegal acts against an unlawful, repressive regime. The public revelation of this secret at this particular time in Israel's troubled history, when violent terrorism had just been the cause of innocent death, was in itself potentially explosive. The teller, in choosing to tell the story, traversed a boundary of normal acceptance and even safety, in the evident hope that the ritual frame would provide a context for understanding. As conductor I did not hesitate to follow through with the enactment of the scene, even though it involved killing. Held by the ritual, actors from the audience enacted this difficult tale as fully as they had the first. This willingness alone was a sign of deep interpersonal acceptance of the teller. Inevitably, there was a flood of response after the enactment; the ritual holding was even more important after the story than before. We enacted many fluid sculptures to express the different reactions of the witnesses. The result was a charged atmosphere. The outcome might well have been chaotic, but the order held—individuals with very diverse perspectives were able, in the playback ritual, to listen to one another. Social discourse took place on a profound level, and the teller for the first time since he had fled to Israel, could stand openly before his neighbors.

Anthropologist Victor Turner uses the word "liminal" to describe how participants in a ritual go to the threshold of normality—and then beyond. His studies in Africa led him to his concept of "social drama," in which community problems are dealt with through ecstatic ceremony. Thus for Turner, rituals, with their departure from everyday order, can create a field for creativity, in which the collective can leap beyond, as it were, what had been possible before. This is what happened in the Israel example. The teller crossed a threshold of disclosure, and carried his listeners with him in the process, such that the audience could regard the pressing social issue of terrorist violence from a fresh perspective, that of the terrorist himself.

This inherent power of the PT ritual is why, despite its flexibility, playback theatre does not always fit into the narrow confines of commissioning organizations, who want to be sure the show is "light," or focuses on team-building, or who want to avoid certain topics. It is also why playback theatre groups can fail—from their own insufficient grasp of heightened dramatic events. It takes a long time to grow into the role of leading playback rituals.

Rituals of transformation, with their climate of bursting possibility, are not risk-free. If the representative of a potential client group grasps the idea of dramatic ritual inherent in playback, she will naturally want an assurance that those leading the ritual have the necessary knowledge to conduct it properly. This is only appropriate.

Often, however, an institutional representative's hesitation comes from a fear of feelings, from the very idea of a heightened event taking place. Then the problem lies with the representative, her institution, and even the society at large, but not, I believe, with the playback actors. Indeed playback theatre will succeed in teaching specific outcomes, such as young people to express themselves more freely or managers to work better together, when the dramatic ritual is allowed to flower fully. In such a case, there may be other far-reaching benefits for the group as well.

Widespread lack of understanding about rituals and their usefulness means that the most crucial part of a playback event often takes place long beforehand, in the planning discussions. Host organizations need to be clear that playback creates a ritual that will stir feelings and respond to problems only indirectly; that everyone present will have an equal voice; and that there is a great potential for creative breakthroughs in these rituals.

More and more institutions are calling on playback theatre to conduct rituals, especially at moments of transition. Examples of such occasions are orientation sessions (beginnings) and retirements (terminations). Playback theatre groups are also called upon at times of crisis, when the need for a strong method as well as a strong container is clear. And playback teams are often called on to perform for a particular group at regular intervals. Thus students in their first week of nursing school could share through PT their feelings about the start of their training, including stories about what inspired them towards nursing. A university faculty department that was being discontinued invited playback to their final party. A married couple in crisis is invited to share their stories in playback, offering each a new way to see the other's perspective. The monthly playback performances, open to all, that are performed by so many companies throughout the world provide a regular place for individuals in their communities to share moments of their lives in an ongoing way. These and many other examples attest to playback's effectiveness in providing groups with a positive way to learn from the past and look to the future.

The Playback Performer's Triad

Let us now turn to the playback practitioners themselves. Jo Salas, in "What Is 'Good' Playback Theatre?" (see page 17), emphasizes that playback theatre is art and shares the task of all art, which is to convey meaning through coherent design, integrity of form, originality, and skill in execution. In this spirit, many playback companies work hard on staging, dynamics, use of metaphor, improvisation, and mastery of the basic PT dramatic forms in order to fulfill their artistic task of creating form for the meaning in a teller's story.

But art alone is not enough. Playback theatre is also an interactive social event, Jo argues, in which much time is spent focusing away from the stage (greeting the audience, introducing the performance, eliciting feelings, invoking stories, interviewing the teller, and so forth). Managing an interactive social event requires a wholly different set of skills. These include good planning and organization, providing the right physical environment, giving those present a chance to be heard, and creating an atmosphere of respect.

Good playback must fulfill the criteria of success in both these realms. Jo concludes that good playback resides in a zone where these elements become indistinguishable from one another.[5] To me this is an important formulation.

Typically playback theatre groups lean towards one side or another. Either they come primarily from an artistic background and are interested in theatrical performing, or they come primarily from a mental health or educational background and are interested more in what we might call the workshop. The former camp has more expressive skills, the latter more group process skills. Sometimes, they even look critically at each other. The "artists" are impatient with process concerns; the "therapists" are disdainful of theatrical elements. Such taking of sides misses the point. All playback practitioners need to develop capacities in *both* domains, no matter what their special interest or emphasis.

If what I have been describing above is true, however, there is a third aspect that is no less important than art and social interaction in creating good playback—ritual. Creating ritual demands different skills yet again: the invocation of a transpersonal dimension, an adherence to rules of conduct; building ecstatic emotional energy; the sparse, rhythmical, highly specialized use of language; and a goal of transformation. To lead the ritual properly, actors focus on their presence on stage. They carefully practice the manner of their listening to the story, setting up a scene, and giving the acknowledgment afterwards. The conductor learns to keep the ritual moving forward, no matter what kind of teller or story; to be a guardian of truth (finding the "deep story"); and to know just when the rules of playback conduct should be adhered to and when they should be relaxed (see diagram).

Thus a good playback actor and leader must be skilled in a triad of roles—as an artist, a host, and a shaman.

This is no light task. It is why serious playback practitioners spend years in apprenticeship and learning.

There are numerous areas where the requirements of these domains seem to place opposite demands on the actors. The art of PT allows aesthetic distance, while the ritual demands involvement. The socially interactive aspect allows for a relaxed, informal contact, while the ritual

ESSENTIAL SKILL AREAS FOR PLAYBACK

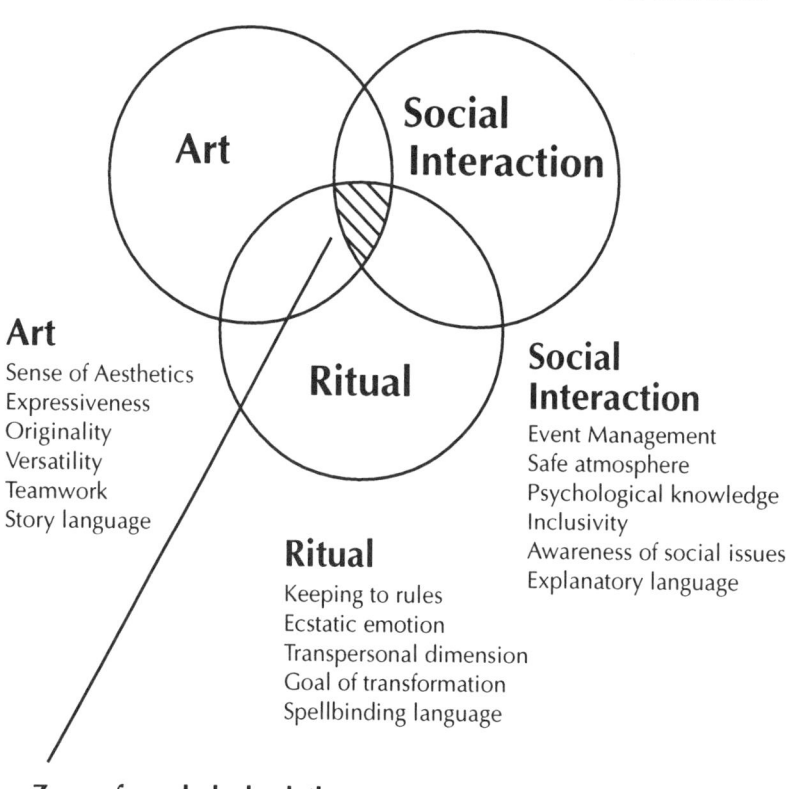

Art
Sense of Aesthetics
Expressiveness
Originality
Versatility
Teamwork
Story language

Ritual
Keeping to rules
Ecstatic emotion
Transpersonal dimension
Goal of transformation
Spellbinding language

Social Interaction
Event Management
Safe atmosphere
Psychological knowledge
Inclusivity
Awareness of social issues
Explanatory language

Zone of good playback theatre

demands transpersonal intensity. It is an objective of the artist to entertain and delight the audience; the host to establish trust and put people at their ease; and the shaman to engender an atmosphere of enchantment and even confusion as a stepping stone to entering what has been called the "other thought."

So how do you plan your opening? Something funny and/or dramatic (artistic)? A clear explanation of what will happen, followed by introductions all around (socially interactive)? Or a slow rhythmical talk, with musical accompaniment, that may not even seem to make much sense (shamanistic)? Clearly, the playback practitioner needs not only to have skills in each domain, but also to be able to blend paradoxical elements effectively. Often, in fact, an opening, while it may lean to one side or another, will accomplish objectives in each of the domains.

If we think of ritual as being a part of this triad upon which the playback experience is based, then there follow certain considerations for the practitioner. I would like to mention some of them here.

First, even though the playback process is spontaneous, the ritual has its rules: The teller must come to the chair; the teller must stay in the chair during the enactment; the teller must tell a personal story. The actors stand when picked for a role; the actors do not talk during the interview. The conductor does not interrupt the enactment; the conductor checks in with the teller after the enactment; the conductor dismisses the teller from the chair. These are *some* of them.

Without the clear framework provided by the rules, spontaneity can quickly turn into chaos, creativity to confusion. With it, the members of the audience feel safe enough to let themselves go into trance, allowing unforeseen breakthroughs.

The need for ritual in playback goes beyond differences between kinds of PT groups, be they professional performing or intimate living room groups. It goes beyond differences in audience size: as much attention must be paid to these formalities with a group of four (teller, conductor, actor, and witness) as with a group of four hundred.

Because of their intensity, rituals place a heavy personal demand on their shamans, and it is essential to take time beforehand to assume the role and afterwards to release it. "Artistic" PT groups sometimes err in modeling themselves on the professional theatre, arriving in time to do a minimum amount of theatrical warming-up and departing as soon as the show is over; while the process-oriented groups sometimes err in trying to give feedback right away and "discuss" the event. Rituals, however, require a specific kind of warm-up and cool down. After being a conductor in playback, for example, it sometimes takes me more than twenty-four hours to return to what I would consider a normal state. And this is after I have been in a state of disturbance for up to two days beforehand.

The idea of playback as service has its locus in this ritual function. Although the artist and the shaman share certain qualities—both are often "called" to their work, for example—there is a fundamental difference. The artist's paramount concern is the creation of his or her art, demanding an ultimate loyalty to personal vision, while the shaman's focus resides in others. In a playback performance, when these roles are in apparent conflict—for instance when the artistic integrity of a show is threatened by a disabled teller whose manner may be slow and halting—there is no doubt in my mind that the shaman role takes precedence. I am not there to look brilliant, or ultimately to create art for art's sake. Nor are the actors. We are there to conduct a process. It has inspired this person to come forward and tell. It is our responsibility to accept the teller and the story fully and to rise to the challenge of creating an atmosphere of deep attention in the audience. Such situations are common in playback, especially when the ritual is strong, for it is then that the isolated feel safe enough to come forward.

Playback's grounding in ritual is perhaps a reason why it can flourish in many different cultures, with different artistic and social traditions. The warm-ups may differ throughout the playback world, and the actors may have very different styles, but the ritual is constant. It provides the safety, and paradoxically, the power.

Life and Death Stories

Playback actors of moderate experience sometimes complain about a particular playback event being dull. "The stories weren't deep," they say. "They were only anecdotes." In time, they will hopefully learn to "hear" the archetypal image inherent in any—even the most mundane-seeming—story. More often than not, however, the sequence of playback stories does contain enough evident seriousness, as well as humor, so that by the end even fledgling actors feel satisfied that indeed, something beneficial has emerged from the void.

Occasionally, however, what we might call a life-and-death story is told, someone's core experience. Then the ritual is most important. At such times the feeling of risk is palpable; there is fear that the teller may "flip out" or that a feeling of chaos may overwhelm everyone.

As an example, I would like to quote from Deborah Pearson, an Australian playback practitioner who has traveled widely. She tells about being guest conductor for a playback performance at a school in Finland when the children had only five minutes before learned about the death of a fellow student in a car accident. If playback is thought of as entertainment, or even as education, one might well argue that this was not the moment for it. Better cancel, and leave the school community to deal as best it can with its shock and grief. If, on the other hand, playback is thought of as a healing ritual, then perhaps it is *just* the moment for it, with one important caveat. It is essential that the company, and especially the conductor, be able to hold the emotions of the crowd and provide a safe place for public mourning.

(Many playback actors know inside themselves that they are not yet ready to contain such strong events, and even if they have the artistic and social interactive skills, they will back away—as they should. And if any of the actors should worry why in their regular performances they are not getting deeper stories from their audiences, it is simply because the audiences sense that the actors are not yet ready to hold them.)

In this particular case, Deborah and her group of Finnish actors, responding to the need for a community healing ritual, did not retreat in the face of community crisis. They went ahead with the performance, ready to enact whatever difficult feelings anyone needed to tell. The young audience responded to the offer of the playback actors. They told about their feelings, and saw them acted out. There were two full stories told and performed. The ritual was accomplished. After the performance, Deborah writes:

> I noticed the heads were not hanging down so much as they left the room, and there was more energy. More of them had cried some tears during the performance. More of them were sitting closer to each other. I felt we had come at exactly the right time to look after them so they had more strength

to continue with their grieving in the next few days and months to come.[6]

There is another important aspect to this ritual holding function in playback. In the excitement of the spontaneous moment, audience members will fail to follow the "rules." One will stand up and criticize the story. Another will want to jump onto the stage. A third will come to the teller's chair and try to manipulate the playback team. At such times the conductor must respond with speed and assurance, knowing when to be permissive and when to be a fierce keeper of the rules. To carry out this task requires not only knowledge and experience, but personal strength and even wisdom.

Shamanic Conducting

One last point: it is important to observe that in order for discourse to take place and liveliness to be enhanced the keepers of the ritual not only need to hold the audience, but sometimes guide it as well. A strong, cohesive group, comprised of autonomous individuals, needs little guidance. They will create just the discourse they need, and find their own sources of liveliness during the course of the event. But in reality, few groups are so enlightened. Problematic individuals are often present, such as the man (it is usually a man) who has *many* comments, *many* feelings, *many* stories to tell. Sometimes the group as a whole is suffering from a belief or attitude that hinders the unfolding of the ritual experience. For example, they may be afraid of feelings, or they may feel that stories are only valid if they have a happy ending. Finally, it is often prevailing views of the society as a whole that can block the process. An example here might be the reluctance of those who consider themselves in any way isolated from the majority—such as an immigrant, a person of color, a very old person—to step up and tell.

In such situations, the playback performers need to have both courage and cleverness in steering around impediments. For example, in spite of playback's core dictum that "anyone can tell," the conductor needs to *manage* (control) the man who wishes to tell too much, so that there will be space for others. The company needs to use all their artistry and humanity, as high practitioners of improvisational theatre and interactive social events, to charm and disarm any group into being open to feelings. They also need to withstand the need for resolution after a sad or painful story, knowing that inherent in their ritual process is the sure promise of transformation. Most importantly, they need always to keep a sharp nose out for prejudice and injustice, which often reveals itself as much from those who are silent as from the lips of those who speak. The ritual demands as much.

It is a commonplace in playback practice that the conductor and players must be "supportive" to the teller, but this idea of the performers as supportive can be clarified by looking at an example of social prejudice. In order to counteract an atmosphere of politeness, or even acceptance of a prejudiced statement or story from the audience, the team will need to exert a fierce allegiance to the idea of social equality. This will involve supporting those isolated or vulnerable *by being tough* with those who voice a prejudicial view. This does not mean casting aspersions; rather it means insisting on what is necessary to keep the ritual constructive.

At a summertime performance on an American university campus, the conductor made immediate contact with a group of African-American teenagers who had arrived together by asking them who they were. Normally it might be thought of as too forward to single out a specific audience group, but in this case contact was preferable to silence and reinforcement of societal patterns of isolation and alienation ("Those black teenagers might cause trouble, let's just ignore them, what are they doing here, anyway.") When one said they were part of a summer job program, the conductor, in preparation for a fluid sculpture, asked him how it was going. At this point, their counselor/supervisor broke in, saying it was going "Wonderfully." Accepting this response, the conductor passed it on to the actors, and they acted out the counselor's "wonderful." But it was important not to leave it at that, for the adult had answered for the (teenage) child. So the conductor repeated the question, saying, "Let's hear from one of the program participants." The risk here on the artistic level was that the actors would get a second "wonderful," and the improvisation might begin to feel boring. On the social level the risk was that *none* of the youngsters would want to speak publicly about how they felt.

What actually happened was that one boy did speak up. He said something interesting and full of feeling, which the actors then made into one of the high points of the show. The conductor's assertiveness paid off, and a prejudice concerning the rights of adults over children was not indulged.

Another example of the shaman as guide took place during the Social Change workshop cited at the beginning of this essay. To recap the situation: there had been two stories told by white participants about the place of blacks in their childhood lives, in which the tellers spoke from the perspective of embarrassed witnesses to prejudice. It was a strong theme. Undoubtedly more whites would come forward with stories that would help them assuage their sense of guilt. At this point, however, I intervened, deliberately asking for a story from one of the two African-Americans. Such intervention runs counter to the basic playback practice, emphasized earlier, of accepting stories from anyone at any time. This was also a request not without risk, for there was a distinct chance that the two singled out might refuse to tell. But the alternative was riskier—repeating an endemic prejudicial pattern of behavior that gave a voice to white, but not black citizens. Thus guidance was essential. In the event, an African-American told. The discourse continued in a constructive direction, towards the hearing of different voices, and vitality had a chance.

Conclusion

For the second performance of our fledgling playback company, more than two decades ago, we made arrangements to visit the children's ward of a general hospital. The staff allowed us to come because they often welcomed volunteers of all sorts, and in their eyes we offered simply entertainment for the children. They had no idea of the ritual power of our form (or they might have had second thoughts). We wore clown-like overalls; we sang a children's song; we were funny and disarming. And yet… since our goal was something more than entertainment, we insisted on performing at visiting hour because we wanted parents to be present. We stuck to our form of inviting individual tellers, even if the bed had to be rolled forward for the child teller to be seen and heard. And we acted out stories—of the children, of the parents, and even the nursing staff. Two memories stand out for me of that day. First, the children told aspects of their experience one sensed they could not tell in ordinary conversation, such as the scary feeling of waiting in a holding room prior to an operation. Second, the experience transformed the atmosphere of the ward: prior to our performance, the children were lethargic and the parents worried behind their comforting smiles. But afterwards, there was eager conversation, and a much lighter mood prevailed that I would even call joyful. It was only our second play-back performance, we hardly knew what we were doing, yet one could feel the power of the playback ritual working.

I came to playback theatre from the pursuit of experimental theatre in the period following the Vietnam War. I thought of myself as a theatre art-ist. In the course of playback's development, I studied psychodrama to learn the group process skills necessary to conduct interactive social events, recognizing how art and social interaction had to be skillfully blended in order to make playback work. Without fully realizing it, I strove during this time to teach my company, my students, and myself the demands of ritual. For it is the ritual component of playback theatre that takes it to our core being, helping us feel newly alive; and it is this ritual component that allows the kind of discourse necessary to transform a dysfunctional or out-worn social order.

It happens through our stories. It happens through dance, image, and music. And it happens because of citizen actors who are willing to learn a challenging art on behalf of their communities.

NOTES

[1] See David Abram, *The Spell of the Sensuous* (New York: Pantheon, 1996); Oliver Sacks, *The Man Who Mistook His Wife for a Hat* (New York: Harper & Row, 1987); Jerome Bruner, *Actual Minds, Possible Worlds* (Cambridge: Harvard University Press, 1986); and Howard Gardner, *Frames of Mind* (New York: Basic Books, 1983).

[2] John Stevenson has written about the habit of playback audiences to remain chatting in the hall after a performance, as if they were attending a celebration. See J. Stevenson, "The Fourth Wall and the Third Space," Independent Study Essay, School of Playback Theatre, 1995.

[3] For more on this subject see chapter three, Preliterary Drama, in my *Acts of Service: Spontaneity, Commitment, Tradition in the Nonscripted Theatre* (New Paltz, NY: Tusitala Publishing, 1994).

[4] See Victor Turner, *Dramas, Fields, and Metaphors* (Ithaca, NY: Cornell University Press, 1974).

[5] See essay beginning page 17 above, and also Jo Salas, *Improvising Real Life: Personal Story in Playback Theatre* (New Paltz, NY: Tusitala Publishing, 1993).

[6] From an article by Deborah Pearson to be published as part of a fifth anniversary volume by Terinateatteri Mielikuva, a playback theatre company in Helsinki, Finland. This volume will also include an early version of this essay on ritual.

EMERGING FROM SILENCE
Uschi Sperling Talks to Jonathan Fox

Uschi Sperling belongs to a playback group in Kassel, Germany. I have known her for a number of years, but only recently learned about her background. Born in 1947, she grew up in the household of her stepfather, a former Nazi officer, who fled the country when Uschi was twelve to avoid imprisonment for crimes against humanity. In the following interview, I talk with Uschi about the challenge of telling her story. What sparked it was Uschi's appearance at the Kassel Symposium bearing a manifesto calling for playback to help heal the wounds of the Nazi past. Meanwhile, she was caught up in her own journey of discovery and healing. In the subsequent year, she learned for the first time of her biological father, now deceased. It turned out that he designed rockets under Werner von Braun, working next to a concentration camp, where, in Uschi's own words, "thousands died under horrible conditions while building the rockets" (he escaped to the East soon after her birth). She also recently met a half sister she never knew she had.

The interview took place in the United States over a three-day period in early winter. Warmed by a wood stove and surrounded by books and old couches, we sat in the room that serves as the School of Playback Theatre office. Present, in addition to Uschi and myself, were Ingo Michler, Uschi's companion and fellow playback company member, and Sarah Urech, who works in the office and belongs to Hudson River Playback Theatre. We spoke English, with occasional exchanges in German.

Even though I was in the role of an "interviewer-conductor" who did not interpose my own tale on the teller, as a Jew I was deeply connected to Uschi's revelations. Nevertheless, I do not think the German-Jewish theme fully explained

135

the emotional tension underlying the earnest tone of our discussion—a tension
that left the four us fully drained after each session. It seemed that merely to dia-
logue about emerging from silence was a challenge that took all our strength.

Uschi: What we experienced in the last fifty or sixty years was the
         duty to be silent. You have to be silent about what you saw
         and what you heard. That is my experience. And we did not
         overcome this yet.

Jonathan: It's very difficult.

U: People think if you don't talk, it goes away.

J: I think it could be that, but often it's not so conscious. It's just so
   painful. The emotions are so complicated.

U: Yes. So what you always hear after the War is, We didn't see and we
   didn't hear anything. That's what people say. And now it's clear that
   in the *Reichskristallnacht* where the Jews were flung out, it happened
   publicly in cities all over Germany.[1]

J: Right. Everyone could see, everyone knew.

U: Psychologically the denial had to do with fear, I can't imagine what
   else it could be. That it could have been you, or you…

J: It raises the question, when you say that, of the future. It can be very
   important to tell the stories of the past, if we think of playback in
   Germany. But it's also very important to bring different people
   together to share their stories, so the *Angst* is less.

U: It could be that a person who tells his or her story in playback
   imagines that in the background there are still the persecutors who
   say, Don't talk, be silent. It's an inner thing. But it could be that the
   person cannot tell because of that.

J: An inner voice.

U: An inner voice, yes. It's not an outer voice, and there is no such
   person, but you may not be able to differentiate it.

J: And that could be dangerous not only because you imagine some
   authority, but also because you could imagine all of your friends and
   colleagues will reject you.

U: But that's what happens when I tell something about it, about my family or my background. People withdraw, just slightly. I experienced it many times, even with friends. So you get an idea that something must be terribly wrong to tell that.

J: It raises this issue of "Do I want to belong? How can I belong?" Everyone has a desire to belong, but in Germany, I feel it's very strong.

U: Sure.

J: This is a loaded question in Germany, because Hitler and the Nazis defined who belonged. The idea of one group belonging is a very complicated, difficult idea.

U: For the second generation after World War II it's a question of "do I want to belong to my parents?" Otherwise "I do not want to belong to my parents, I do not want to belong to Germany, I do not want to belong to the history. I want to be elsewhere. And then I'm homeless."

J: At the Kassel Symposium you gave me a written statement, with a sentence in it where you say that as a member of the second generation and as a stepdaughter of a Nazi, you know what it's like to need and want to be quiet. I want you to comment on that statement, which feels very important.

U: Nobody told me to be quiet, not my father, not my mother—but I felt it all the time, that things were going on in our family which were not exactly unusual, but that we shouldn't tell about. I always experienced that something was going on. Something was wrong. Even though I didn't think in those terms. Somehow I got to know that my father—when I say father, I mean my stepfather, but I was raised by him, I was one and a half when he came into our family and so I grew up with him as my father... I sensed that there was something coming, that my father had to go to prison. But we, the other children and I, we didn't really know. All we knew was that there were people whose first names we knew, who crowded into our house each night and they had big discussions with my father. Two of them turned out to be the daughter and wife of an important

Nazi. And others had no names, though afterwards I learned who they were. And then the feeling rose, someday I will read in a book the name of my father. And I will find him in a history lesson.

J: You told me later that you did read about him in a newspaper.

U: Yes, it really happened, but that was not until twenty years later, in the seventies. I read in the newspaper that he was going to prison to serve a lifelong sentence. The main feeling in my childhood was that there were things going on which were strange and were not talked about, and we breathed it in as children.

J: In the statement that you wrote and gave to me at the Symposium, you talked about the importance of doing playback in those very places, you called them the shadow places, where the Nazi past was most alive. I read this in the rush of the Symposium, and I thought, this is very important and what does Uschi want to do with this. Perhaps she wants to stand up and read it to everyone. I was very impressed but didn't know what this would mean. Then you surprised me by saying, "Well, no, it's OK, I don't need to do anything with it." I put it on the bulletin board for people to look at, but I don't think many people saw it. So my next question is, why didn't you want to do more with it?

U: (breathless laughter) Yes, that's the same history, it's the same history that I was saying earlier. To step forward, to say, You must talk about that, especially in Germany… If you have a Symposium in Germany you must talk about the past. If not that theme, what else then, in Germany? But then *Angst* comes, and all these ghosts come and tell me I should not. I mean I'm not psychotic, but somehow it was impossible to do it. My anxiety was that nobody wanted to hear it. And so I withdrew. And I felt very bad during the whole Symposium, because I felt I took a step forward, and then I went two steps back. I was unhappy about it. I needed to not stand alone. To stand alone, that's the terrible thing. I feel that this theme is not welcome, it's not at all welcome. It's hard to know if I really do stand alone or if it is just my fear about it.

J: I think what you're saying is very important for playback everywhere. How can we as playback actors and conductors encourage that voice to speak which feels alone? There are so many people who do feel alone and stay quiet.

U: You talked about the Maori people, and how a Maori never stands alone. This sentence impressed me most, because I felt that with this theme, you cannot stand alone. At the Symposium, I wrote my paper alone, at night, and I didn't inform anybody. The words just came. I didn't discuss it.

J: There's a process over the last few years of not only your personal discoveries, but of our playback meetings—yours and mine— beginning with when we first met four years ago in a workshop. Then there was the Symposium in 1997. Our next meeting after that was this past May in Bad Bevensen a year later, where you were about to begin the two-week playback Practice course. At the last minute, you decided not to participate, and you explained to me later why. Perhaps you could say now, why did you decide not to take the Practice course?

U: I was just at the important point in my personal search for my family, where I really came from. I was on the point of meeting my sister whom I just had found.

J: This is the sister from your biological father, not your stepfather.

U: Yes, not my stepfather.

J: When you wrote your original statement, you didn't even know about your father.

U: No, I didn't even know. After that paper, my search speeded up. I went to the concentration camp where my father worked as an engineer, just next to the camp. That was a terrible discovery, that both fathers were so deeply involved.

J: Your sister is from his second family, after the war, which you didn't know about.

U: Yes, I didn't know anything about it until that time. My father committed suicide when he was forty-one, really young, in 1961. I knew when I went to my sister, and talked with her, that the history would come out. In my sister's family they never talked about his death till I came. And so I was very afraid that I could fling her into a very, very stressful thing. Just before I came to Bad Bevensen, I'd been having a kind of symptom where I thought my brain was not OK, so I'd had examinations of my head, and it turned out that it was totally all right.

J: So you were actually having physical symptoms, because of all this.

U: Yes, I thought that maybe I had a brain tumor. At least it all had to do with my question, am I normal? Do I want to see all of it? Or are the others normal, who still want to be silent about it?

J: I'm interested in what stories we hesitate to tell in playback, or what stories may not be possible in playback, or what are the limitations of playback. What do we still need to discover in order to make play-back useful for the most important stories? You obviously felt that this playback training was not right for you at that time. Part of it was the raw feelings you were having, and even some physical symptoms you were having. Were there other reasons, too, why you hesitated to participate?

U: Yes, it was an unfamiliar group. I mean there were some very familiar people in it, and you were somehow familiar as well, but I didn't know the group as a whole. And what I did not know was, how do they think about those themes? What did they experience? I know from the discussions that when that theme comes up, then hate comes and very strong rejection, very strong feelings. And so in an unknown group you must have a certain safety. The question is, how could you be safe? Who creates safety? And about this theme, I think there is no consensus that we want to talk about it.

J: You said to me when we took a walk (because you stayed there at Bed Bevensen, though not in the group) that you were not sure whether the other participants really wanted to hear your story, and whether it would be possible to carry on as a training if these kinds of stories were told. I didn't have an answer. It could be true that your story would be not welcome in the training. Of course I'm a visitor, I'm a stranger to this context.

Something happened during the training that was very strange, but also interesting. Some of the students were about to perform, and an actor with a tambourine was bringing in the "audience"—the other students and me. We'd been having coffee while they got ready, and you'd been there with us. This actor with the tambourine brought you into the room, even though you hadn't been officially participating. So here was the playback performance team with the student audience as expected, with this other person who everybody knew but who was not part of the class, there in the back. And the conductor didn't ask her anything. I noticed this. After about twenty minutes or so you left. When we were discussing the performance later, I asked the conductor, "What about that other member of the audience?" The conductor said, "Well, I noticed her, but I didn't know what to do." For me it was a significant moment, because there often is somebody there in the shadows, so to speak. The conductor may hesitate, because if you make a strong invitation to that person, something may come that is very, very strong, and in fact may be too strong. So this conductor may have hesitated, because asking you, "How are you, what do you have to say, what is your story?" would have brought this theme to this performance. So you were not asked anything, and you left.

U: Yes. It's a question, if there is someone like me who really is into something, and can no longer make a calm choice—"OK, I'll tell this story and not that"—because he's so deeply into it that he simply has to bring it out, when he is invited. What happens then?

J: So you need to feel not only safe, you need to trust that the playback team has the strength, the knowledge to help you bring out the story in a way that's going to feel all right. And that's a very big challenge.

U: The first time I experienced playback, four years ago, I told something of my very early childhood, and you were the conductor.

J: I remember the story.

U: I had never told that before. I had the feeling that just you and I were there, and nothing else, and I told it to you, and you listened. That was enough. Then afterwards there was the performance, which was very good. But the first thing was the dialogue, the interview, and for me that was the core. But the memory of this experience didn't help later in that moment at Bad Bevensen.

J: Well, there's one more moment in this sequence of our meetings in playback. A couple of weeks after Bad Bevensen I led a two-day playback workshop with two Kassel groups, your group and the university group. During that weekend, stories of the Nazi past began to come up. I suggested to the group that we explore how to portray these stories. My sense was that the group had very mixed feelings about how—and whether—to explore this. It was a very, very tender subject. But we did, and I still don't know how useful it was, because I'm not sure how much people really wanted to do this. When you have a story that has a Nazi element in it, or a war element in it, what are the different levels at which we can do it, what are the choices you can make?

I did ask you on the second day of that weekend if you wanted to tell part of your story. I asked you privately. And you agreed. I'll just share one or two of my impressions of that, and then of course you can give yours. You told about meeting your sister—you had just had this very important meeting over Easter—and it was a wonderful story of coming together, a meeting of these two sisters, half-sisters who had never met, one from the West and one from the East. Naturally, your father was a character. He embodied the Nazi past, and it was a very important part of your story. A young actor played your father. My impression was that although he was doing his best, he was quite frozen in that role. It was very difficult for him. It was a case where the actors couldn't fulfill the story, much as they tried. I've had that experience elsewhere in Germany and in other places, when a story touches so much the collective story that actors find it very difficult to fulfill the role.

That time you were able to choose your story carefully, I felt.

U: Yes, that's right.

J: And yet even so, it was collectively not easy to play your story back. Even though it was just a very small part of it, almost a happy part of it.

U: I remember that I did not describe my father. I mentioned him, sure, he was our father, but I did not say much about him. Listening to you now, I ask myself: if you had asked me to say more about him, what would have happened? The story would have switched totally. It would have gone to my father, and not to my sister. But I'm sure that I would not have told it.

J: Right. I feel that a very important strength of playback is its gentleness, in the sense that it's fine to tell just that part that you want to tell. Even though there's more. Often in playback we're going to tell just a small part.

U: I remember how my father was on the stage. The actor had a cloth on his head, and you could not see the face. And for me, watching, it was a very strong picture. I would not have said that this guy did not fulfill the role. You could not see his face because of the cloth over it. And that's a reality, too. I never looked my father in the face, I never met him. There are so many things in the dark with him. It was a strong picture, a strong image for what really was in the family as well.

J: It's very good to hear that correction.

U: That picture reminds me that you have to look more. Yes?

J: Yes, exactly.

U: So it's not fulfilled, you have to look more, to see what it's about.

J: You've been a member of a playback group, and you share stories with each other. Are you able to share this part of your life story?

U: No, no.

J: Why not? Because there are people in other groups, not only in Germany, that have this question. Can we tell our story in our playback group? What kind of playback group do we have? I have always felt that a first step for a playback group is to be able to share their own stories.

U: I agree. But somehow I think this theme is different. It would be one thing to tell about my father's suicide, which is terrible enough, but

143

to say, "My father saw thousands and thousands of people dying. He must have seen it, because he was so near. And he worked for all this, he worked for it"—that's different.

It is a huge step to tell.

J: One argument people may have is, Let's not even try to use playback with these kinds of stories. Let's focus on the present and creating playback for all kinds of voices, but voices of now, not necessarily voices of the past—especially the collective past.

U: No, I don't agree, because I know from psychodrama that when things are told, then you can forget. And I know also that theatre works on a subconscious level. The hope is that when you tell the story, it could change something in your subconscious, then you could forget.

J: Yes, and of course when you say forget, it's not that you necessarily forget…

U: …no, not at all.

J: You let go of…

U: release…

J: …release some of the parts that are so heavy. And actually I believe that that kind of freedom enables you to be much more creative about the present and the future.

U: The big thing I didn't talk about yet is the shame. That's bigger than fear. And when shame disappears, then you are free. And you do not forget it, but you do not feel the shame about what you went through and where you came from.

J: Do you have any thoughts about how playback might be used better for helping people tell these kinds of stories?

U: One thing I have learned is that you *can* tell your story, even if you are afraid. You won't die. When I say this it maybe seems silly, but it's really a question of "Am I alive afterwards?" I think that's a signal for all the other tellers, that it *is* possible to tell and stay alive.

J: One idea is to find a way to make it possible for people to tell just a small part.

U: Yes, a very small part.

J: Not need to tell the big stories. That's a first step. I feel that an acting team can do such a skillful job of doing just a small part of it and suggesting more, or having symbols of more. Indirect, but very powerful.

U: Because what playback can do is to show the other elements which are not told. Like in my very first story four years ago about being a child in a house that was bombed. You could see through the walls. In the scene, as the company played it, I was in bed and I could see the stars. It gave me something completely new to think about. OK, I grew up in a terrible time, but there was also freedom as a possibility. The damage of Germany, the damage to the houses which was terrible, but there was also a possibility to change it all. And the playback company showed it... you could see the stars.

In that story, in different ways, the actors knew more than I told, and they knew more than you asked. And they showed more than I think they even knew. They invented a figure whom I never mentioned, a figure who was indeed in my history, a soldier who walked down the street homeless. And that was the story of my stepfather. He was homeless and then he came into our family, married my mother. The actors were totally right. And I think they could never have created it by thinking about it, they just acted.

J: That was a wonderful moment.

U: Yes, it was... What I'm thinking about now is if you make a strong or specific invitation to someone, as you did with me in the Kassel workshop this year—as opposed to the more normal, Who wants to tell the next story?—what are the consequences?

J: It's a very good question. As the conductor you may know something about the story beforehand, but often you don't. I sometimes make a very strong invitation just from intuition. But is it a good thing? I know that as I get more experience as a conductor, and have more confidence that I know the playback method, I do make strong invitations. If there is someone in the audience whose voice is not heard, someone who I feel is not comfortable to speak, I may make very strong invitations. It's very risky, because if it's not done well, this person is going to feel much worse. I feel it is important to evaluate whether it was good or not. I don't think we can say that it's always great to come and tell your story, or it's always great to invite someone to come. Because they may feel worse.

U: Yes, because it's maybe too early, a too early birth, and that is dangerous.

J: A premature birth. And the audience also may not be able or willing to hear. As an American conducting in Germany, I often feel, "Well who am I to invite a story like this?" Yet on the other hand, maybe it's good for someone not so caught in the culture to be the conductor. And we can do that for each other, perhaps. Because each culture has its own stories that are so difficult.

U: Yes. I think it has a kind of logic. I mean I'm now here in America, telling you my story, and I didn't tell it in my playback group in Germany.

J: Do you feel the same way a year later about performing playback in the shadow places?

U: No, I feel differently now. Because in the meantime I saw that concentration camp where my father worked. You can still see parts of the rockets which were built there, which my father worked on. They were produced there in this *Bergwerk*. You see even the toilets, and other things which are still there. When you really feel what happened there, you are silent. You cannot tell a story, you cannot even speak. Because all these eyes of dead people look at you. It's somehow to do with dignity, I don't know. You should not speak. At least not us, perhaps. Maybe the victims have to have a voice there. Or later generations, but not us. Maybe it's the same as that you as an American come to conduct, and then it's maybe possible to speak, because there's distance.

J: Do you have other ideas about how we can shape or design playback so that people are comfortable telling the hidden stories?

U: Yes. As I mentioned before, I think the interview is especially important. So that it begins with two people, not the whole group. To create a kind of commitment and relationship. Which is maybe the grounding for the teller.

J: I've come to feel that the concept of performance in a public setting, lasting two hours, is perhaps not the best concept. That we need a different concept, something longer, something perhaps not public in that way. But what that should be, I'm not so clear yet.

U: I'm not so clear either. What makes sense is maybe to have interruptions, to have breaks and then meet again. Ja?

J: Ja.

U: And in the break, there happens so much. And there is a *Bogen*—an arc or a curve that spans several days. So that the people who join this have a feeling of flowing, a kind of river, that there are stories flowing, *fliessen*... and that they are in a kind of stream. They become more and more familiar with the stories and with each other. I think it is very important, that afterwards they are able to go alone, back into their own setting.

J: Do you mean that afterwards they will feel stronger, and more empowered?

U: Yes. To stand alone.

J: To stand alone in their own setting. And not have to be quiet.

U: Yes, realizing that they have a special and difficult theme, but that they are enabled to speak more. That's a big goal. But that could happen. When the shame goes away.

J: Yes.

U: Usually we think that for the teller the most important thing is to see his or her story on the stage, but for the teller it can be enough that he or she just tells. And for the audience it's good to see it enacted, and then to be able to tell more.

J: But also I think it could be important for the teller that the audience sees the story enacted, then the audience can connect much more strongly to the teller.

U: Yes.

J: So that connection is also part of the whole process. But you're saying that the most important part for the teller is just that first telling. I understand that. For many people, that walk to the chair, and saying, "This is my story, I don't have a beginning or an end or a shape, but it's about this"—that's what is most important.

U: That's what's most important. Because she steps out from the family history of silence into another history. She steps really out of that, leaves it behind and goes to the chair, and leaves the whole family history behind.

J: What was it like for you in this respect, when you told your story?

U: At first I was so much involved with telling that I could not look at the enactment. In the beginning I did not see anything.

J: When you talk about a meeting that might last three days, and have many pauses, where there would be this *Bogen*, you could easily have just a telling, and act it out later.

U: Yes, that's a good thing. That makes sense, because what I experienced is that I could not see the scene at first. I began to pay attention somewhere in the middle. Because it's so *aufregend*—stirring, stimulating.

The other thing is, what could be the ending?

J: The performance concept says that after two hours, you bring it to an end and it's over. My feeling here is that there is an aftermath, and the playback group and the playback leaders have responsibility for afterwards also. The ending needs to be longer. It's not enough that you tell and watch, and then we forget about you. There has to be some way that we stay in touch, or we take some responsibility. It's not therapy. And yet we need a concept where we do stay in touch.

U: Somehow.

J: Somehow.

U: What just comes to mind is that the Jewish people say, "Next year in Jerusalem," and in German we say *"Auf Wiedersehen,"* see you again. It could be something that gives a feeling that there will be more. Maybe to have another ritual.

J: A ritual, both a ritual of ending, but also of continuance. Of course playback does continue, one of the characteristics of playback is that the groups stay together year after year. And they often are part of a community year after year. It does continue, but it's not necessarily part of the concept or the theory.

U: Maybe that's not a thing you can discuss and create, maybe it's just a group dynamic thing. I'm not talking about a happy ending, but finding a closing that is right. What does the group need? Do they want to talk to the actors maybe, afterwards, or to the conductor?

J: There must be then a place for that. The actors must be ready and willing.

U: Another point in my Symposium statement is about the dialogue between the generations—to make it possible for the second genera- tion and the third generation to come into contact. So that they can ask each other now, although they've never asked, or dared to ask, their parents. Maybe in a playback audience it's possible. I experi- enced this in the Kassel workshop with the mixed group—the students and the members of my own group. Afterwards many of the young people asked me all about my family and what I'd learned. I think there was a big need to ask. Maybe they had never asked their mothers and fathers, though they kind of knew that this all happened.

J: It helped them to hear your story, and to be there, to be part of it. And it helps the teller too, because they don't say, "We wish you had not told." They say, "Tell us more."

U: Yes. That's also an aspect of how we end; maybe there should be a possibility of being asked for more, if someone is willing to tell more than he tells on the chair. I never expected that there would be so many questions. And I know from myself when older people from the first generation after the war tell something, I get such big ears, I want to have more, because I never could ask my parents. And that's a thrill.

J: To have open communication between the generations. I think playback has some good possibilities, because it is able to show stories that are very complex. The answer does not need to be simple. When people accept the playback idea, there's room for many different opinions or many different feelings. People can watch without needing to say what's right or wrong, in the sense that playback accepts anybody's feeling and the enactment doesn't need to say, this is true, or this is not true.

U: It takes a special courage of the actor to show the ugliness, to act the hard roles.

J: Of course, of course. And when the group is too politicized, playback cannot happen.

U: That's right. And this theme *is* political. But it's also a situation where the story is only a story, and the teller is just the teller. It's not a proclamation.

J: …it's not an argument.

U: It's only a story. And there is the ritual, a teller tells his story, and there is silence, not a discussion.

J: Sometimes the ritual might break down. Somebody will say, "No." If it is too strong we cannot do playback. We can have an argument, maybe.

U: Sure, that can happen as well. And maybe that is not a mistake. It's part of the stream, it's now the time for the argument. I think it will be clear in the first minutes if this is an event where the accepted opinion takes precedence or if there are other possibilities. This will be decided in the first moments.

J: How in the first moments can you create an atmosphere where all parts of the story can be voiced?

U: Yes, yes. It's not so easy but it's very important, I think. It's a sign of what's really going on. When it's a story about Nazis in the family it has to be about human beings, not stereotypes. The most terrible thing for us in my generation is to realize that the fathers who we knew and loved and who were good in some ways also took part in evil. And that they are one person. The actor has to be that one person. But it's not so easy to show both these sides.

J: I think the actor needs to practice that, how to be that kind of man.

U: Yes, to have these two sides. Which is human as well. It's not just a Nazi theme. There are both sides in all of us. To dare to show them is very important in those stories, I think. A teller may or may not tell both sides. But I think the way he tells, you at once know that there is another side.

One thought I don't know where to put: somehow we have to honor those persons who were really killed. We all survived; we are not the victims.

J: Perhaps in a performance or an event that focuses on these stories there would always be a place to honor those who did die. So that they are part of our memory, and part of our story, always.

U: Yes, it must be, somewhere in the room or on the stage. There should be no confusion. We are aware that we are not the victims and we do not forget about them.

It is a question of the *Würdigung* [dignity] of the people who are not there, the actual victims. And then there is the question of place—where can the story be honored as a story? So it can become a story among many such stories.

J: The basic idea of playback is an aesthetic one, that the beauty can hold the most difficult truth and make it possible for us to see. That's what art can do. Playback theatre is part of the oral tradition. Stories live in our memories and our hearts.

U: Maybe you don't have to worry so much about finding a good ending, because there never can be a good ending. But you have to worry about how it might continue, and what you can do to create continuity, because this story is also a story about broken continuity in Germany.

J: To come back to the question of what it's like for actors to be in such stories—actors can be torn between serving the teller and their own feelings. It may be hard for them to be present.

U: I have no answer, but I think that it could happen that you simply could not be on stage, that you are maybe close to the teller or close to someone in the audience and you're concerned about them.

J: It could take some special sense of permission for the actors to do what they needed to do. Maybe not act. Or perhaps they could show their feelings, including the feeling of wanting to disappear. Because it might be a feeling that the teller has too and doesn't express.

U: Before I mentioned that I think the most important step is from the audience to the teller's chair. And the teller or the potential teller has to do that alone, just for himself. He has to do this very hard work, somehow, to go to the chair, to stand up for his story. And I asked myself about ending. How could the story or the play come to a really good end? Because even if it's a terrible story it should come to a good place to end. And I was thinking that the way back from the teller's chair to the audience again must not be alone. Someone from the audience could come to take the teller back into society.

J: So that Maori idea again, not to be alone.

U: First the teller has to be alone, to come to the chair.

J: But leaving the chair, not to be alone...

U: That's right. Someone from the audience, from society, gives her hand or his hand, and says, "Come back to us."

J: Yes, I like that idea.

U: The other idea is that maybe after the actors stop, the music can go on. That the music ends it. The actors are on the stage, and the music still plays as long as the teller is returning to the audience and maybe for a little bit afterwards.

J: I would think that it should work well, that idea.

U: The other thing I thought about is the victims who are maybe not mentioned, but who are part of the story. Once, when I was in a story but not in a role, I spontaneously played one of the people who were killed. It was not in fact a good choice—I was lost on the stage, I couldn't express what I wanted to say. My idea was that the victims, who were what the story was all about, should be there in the background. But it was so hard to express that.

J: You were feeling your way, but the other actors weren't with you really. It wasn't something you were all trying together. I think that actors need to practice that.

U: As I have said, there must be some way to give the dignity back to victims, there must be a corner on the stage, or a familiar symbol, so we all know what we are talking about.

Earlier you mentioned this playback scene where my father was on the stage with my sister and me. And you asked me what my impression was, and I said that the actor's choice to cover his face with cloth was true for me. It reminded me that I have to go further. So many things are still hidden, such as the meaning of my father's suicide. After I saw the enactment, I thought that maybe he did it to join the dead. I imagined he did it so he could lay beside the victims of the concentration camp next to which he worked.

I know that I'll never find the true answer, but I can achieve the *Annäherung daran.* I can get closer. And so somehow this thought gives him some dignity back. And me also.

Uschi (reading the interview three months after being on Jonathan's "teller's chair"):

My first concern was to find a "good place," where I could feel safe enough to tell my story. Germany seemed too close, somewhere else in Europe too strange. So the interview took place "in between," where it was both—familiar and strange. Without Jonathan's strong and friendly invitation, I would not have taken a seat on the "teller's chair." The feeling of being torn between fear and shame about my family history would probably have won and left all hope of release and transformation behind. In this situation I needed someone who was determined to hear the story.

Interviews with the first, second, and third generation families of Holocaust survivors, as well as families of Nazis and Nazi sympathizers, show that the wounds are not verheilt, that they still hurt and poison lives. It is obvious that time does not heal and that the healing process has to have outside helpers. If and how playback theatre can be such a helper is one of my questions.

In the interview I was in different roles. On the one hand I told some parts of my story; on the other hand I discussed playback theatre possibilities from a more distanced point of view. Changing between the levels was not easy, and perhaps at times confusing.

I would like to thank you, the audience, and leave the teller's chair. Now I give it to you.

Note

[1] In November 1938 on Kristallnacht, or the "Night of Broken Glass," Nazis burned down synagogues, smashed windows of Jewish shops, and arrested many Jews. –Ed.

Playback Portrait

LINDA PARK-FULLER
USA

It was a review of Fox's book, *Acts of Service: Spontaneity, Commitment, Tradition in the Nonscripted Theatre* that caught the eye of Linda Park-Fuller. A professor in the department of theatre and dance at Southwest Missouri State University, she had already discovered the interactive work of Augusto Boal. But playback theatre seemed to emphasize *story,* and she liked that.

Less than six years later, she has been twice to New York for training and is active in pursuing playback theatre on a number of fronts.

The student company she runs out of her department, BareStage, specializes in interactive, improvisational theatre. About half their work is playback, and the rest is based on Forum Theatre and trigger scripts (monologues and scenes designed to "trigger" discussions). Originated in 1993, BareStage performs in community settings as well as on campus. For instance, they have performed for middle school students, a breast cancer support group, and a homeless shelter.

Asked about what it is like being a professor and leading a student playback group, Linda, aged 50, replied: "The double role as group member and leader is perhaps more pronounced in an educational setting, where the authority of the teacher is traditionally high." She discusses this subject of "role straddling" with the group, trying to be clear about who will make what kinds of decisions, and she also makes sure to spend time with them in social settings.

Linda's department organized the 1997 Ozark/Flint Hills Performance Festival, an intercollegiate interactive theatre event that featured playback. Most of the participants came from theatre programs in the Midwest. At least two collegiate playback groups have developed from that seed, at the University of Northern Iowa and at Eastern Michigan University.

As well as her work with BareStage, Linda has brought playback into her ongoing research, which has centered on literary and oral narrative. In the past three years, she has presented papers on "Re-Valuing the Oral Tradition in Higher Education: PT in the Academy" and "Playback Theatre And Psychooncology: Performed Ethnography In The Arena Of Health Care," and along with her PT colleagues in Iowa and Michigan, "Playback Theatre: an Innovative and Ancient Communication Tool and Art Form." She also participated in a panel on "The Ethics of Interactive Theatre."

Speaking about her scholarly work, Linda says she is fascinated with how the narrative form, "our native literary genre," functions. She is interested in studying how personal narrative can move people to make behavioral changes. "Playback provides ways for self-expression in ways I've just not seen available before. This helps people. It moves people. And it involves the audience as scripted theatre can't do. I'm interested in that." In the future, Linda hopes to continue with her research and BareStage, "doing even more playback than we do now." She also hopes one day to be part of a playback company outside the university.

Linda speaks about her experience with BareStage at the homeless shelter, and one girl in particular who told a story about her violent father. The children in such facilities, she explains, are often there for a very short time because their mothers are evading their batterers. Thus they do not have a community. Linda recounts how the kids shone under the attention of the young college students, who took them so seriously and acted out their stories. Especially this one little girl. After the performance, Linda said to the counselor, "At least she has you to be with her and help her." The counselor replied, "This might be all she gets, but it will help."

For Linda, it all goes together, the scholarly research, her own development as a member of a playback company, and reaching out to others—activities that take place on campus, and off.

HOW PLAYBACK THEATRE WORKS
A Matter for Practical Research

Heinrich Dauber [1]

"People and countries serve as mirrors for each other. They are also, of course, themselves, just as a mirror is itself and not that which it reflects. However, they seldom recognize what they are in reality: mostly they see that which is hidden deep inside only within a reciprocal reflection. To differentiate between the 'mirror' and 'reflection,' when in addition reflected in the multifaceted realm of a living mind and a human being, is not easy. This ability to keep the reflector and reflection separate is so poor and relatively undeveloped in us, that in times to come they will undoubtedly laugh at us as we laugh at monkeys." [2]

—*Laurens van der Post*

After almost twenty-five years of successful playback theatre practice in over thirty countries around the globe, in completely different cultures as well as social contexts, it does not seem too soon to turn our attention to the question, How does playback theatre work?, long posed by the founder of playback theatre:

> There is need for research: to develop new methods for the documenta-
> tion and analysis of oral theatre; to study the levels of context-text related
> communication as they become manifest in an improvisational perfor-
> mance; to examine the spontaneous creative process of the improvisational
> actor (the results might have usefulness far outside the field of theatrical
> studies). Most needed are historical and comparative studies of nonscripted
> theatre. These should include studies of the transition between preliterary
> and literary as well as the interstices between literary and postliterary
> genres. Exactly what actual connections have there been between the vari-
> ous NST (nonscripted theatre) practitioners, both horizontally and
> vertically? I am fascinated by what appears to be a central European hot
> spot in the germination of the NST movement: were the progenitors
> Goethe, Laban, Brecht, Moreno, and colleagues as yet unknown?[3]

The University of Kassel, in the form of an academic symposium on playback theatre, took up this wish from Jonathan Fox in May of 1997. It was done, not as so often is the case in the relationship between science and practice, as an expression of scientific hegemonic desire, but as an "act of service" towards the worldwide playback movement.

That such a symposium did not take place earlier can be attributed in part to the fact that it was only possible after the publication of Jo Salas's book, *Improvising Real Life*,[4] which informed a wider audience of the fundamental aims and principles of playback theatre. Jonathan Fox himself in his own ground-breaking book, *Acts of Service*, which was written earlier but published later, remained caught up in an apologetic argument towards the established theatre and theatre criticism in the US. As he said, their "iron grip on a literary orientation of theatre" and their steadfast refusal to recognize playback theatre and other forms of NST is unfortunate, but nevertheless should not justify the ongoing separation of playback theatre and text-oriented theatre. This would miss the core of the matter for Jonathan Fox. Playback theatre is more than just nonscripted theatre. In fact, the uniqueness of playback theatre is based far more on the moral standards of combining spontaneity and service. In his conclusion, Fox expresses it this way: "For me, what is most important is to create a theatre that is neither sentimental nor demonic, hermetic nor confrontational, but ultimately a theatre of love." [5]

But can a "theatre of love" be researched? And what are the fundamental questions? One thing seems certain to me. The international playback movement is not dependent on research, any more than the international theatre and art scenes are. Nevertheless, as soon as it makes sense to incorporate playback theatre as an integral part of studies in teaching, therapy, or social work,[6] or when training is offered, as at the School of Playback Theatre in New York, Germany, and Japan, then the necessity arises to legitimize these institutions. Therefore, the discussion about researching playback theatre is to be established within an academic and institutional context.

The most general question, often posed by playback theatre practitioners as well as by outsiders, is simply, How does playback work? In a German context this question sounds something like this, "How is it that the players bring to the stage things they cannot possibly know and yet precisely correspond to the storyteller's experience? That scene must have been talked about in advance. It cannot work any other way."[7]

Many, including experienced practitioners of playback theatre, hold the opinion that this question can only be answered intuitively, rather than scientifically. As a playback practitioner myself, I am partially inclined to agree. However, as a social scientist, I do not share this perspective, because in my view it is based on a restricted positivistic view of science.[8]

The Four Questions
For the purpose of research I choose the following (tentative) definition: *playback theatre is both an **individual** as well as **collective** experience, which on the one hand can only be understood from a **subjective perspective**—i.e., through (individual and collective) self-reflection, and on the other hand can be described from an **objective perspective** as an objective experience of a theatre performance in a particular social context.*

Let me give an example. During the weeks of a strike at the University of Kassel in December 1997, playback performances from various groups were held on the subject "Strike." At one of these performances, in which German students told about the strike, the conductor asked an Iranian to talk about his experience striking under the Shah and Khomeini. The brief, mostly implicit story was highly dramatic and deeply moving for everyone present from the following different perspectives:

From the *individually subjective perspective* the story was very present for the teller. On this day, for the first time after many years, he had again taken part in a demonstration, and he had told his story for the first time in public.

From the *collectively subjective perspective* there arose a long discussion within the group and with other playback players who had seen the performance, whether and to what extent this kind of dramatic story can be publicly performed.

From the *individually objective perspective* the players, particularly the main character, succeeded intuitively in portraying the decisive focus of the story in an artistic manner ("I go out. I take part. And I will go out again").

From the *collectively objective perspective* these stories and their enactment changed the entire atmosphere among the students and engendered a new understanding of the meaning of the strike. It would express itself in the weeks to come in the students' treatment of one another.

From this, four dimensions arise for research hypotheses:

content dimension individually subjective perspective	**artistic dimension** individually objective perspective
ritualistic dimension collectively subjective perspective	**social dimension** collectively objective perspective

These dimensions can be formulated as simple questions: What does playback theatre achieve or how does it 'work' from the perspective of the storyteller? (upper left) What does playback theatre 'achieve' or how does it 'work' in regard to the ritual interaction between the storyteller, conductor, players and audience? (lower left) What makes a performance artistically effective? (upper right) What effect does playback theatre have on the audience, the performing company (i.e. the troupe of players, musician, and conductor) and on the social context in which it is embedded? (lower right)

The difficulty in adequately describing such a complicated event as playback theatre, or even in examining its 'effectiveness', becomes immediately apparent, because the 'effectiveness' cannot be generally determined. Rather each dimension must be judged by its own criteria. Which criteria of effectiveness should count as valid in regard to the storyteller; to the interaction between the storyteller, conductor, players, and audience; to the theatre troupe; and to the social context, and so forth?

In addition, none of these dimensions can be discussed in isolation without mentioning their relationship to the other dimensions. To be precise, it is not about the effects of single variables, but rather about their common intersection—i.e., the interaction between different effects—content *and* ritual, ritual *and* artistry, artistry *and* social interaction.

Once again, let us review the four questions:

What does playback theatre achieve and how does it work from the perspective of the storyteller? In my opinion, this question can only be examined based on criteria such as *subjective sincerity, congruence, and authenticity.* The aim is to recognize the *personal meaning* of the story, to discover its overt (conscious) and covert (unconscious) themes and possibly, by portraying it on stage, to broaden the meaning of the story for the teller. The only valid statement from this perspective is an "I-statement," such as "That's exactly what I experienced." Drawing on the example presented earlier of the Iranian student teller, "I go out again and will not let myself be oppressed, not in school, not at the university, nor in my private life."

What does playback theatre achieve or how does it 'work' in regard to the ritual interaction between the storyteller, conductor, players, and audience? This question can only be examined based on criteria such as *mutually subjective appropriateness* and *mutual understanding.* The aim is to discover the collective meaning of the story for the group, for the community, and in the process to deepen understanding. From this perspective the group can formulate "we-statements," such as "We are shaped by the same experience," or, "We are affected by a very similar fate." In the example, the last storyteller of the performance posed the question, "What does the strike mean for us? Is it a game or an existential challenge?"

What makes a performance artistically effective? This question (and the fourth) can be relatively objectively examined based on criteria such as precision in representation. The aim is to portray the story and its various aspects for the storyteller, the audience, and the players in an artistically appropriate and sophisticated manner. Based on our example (from the view of the storyteller): "Today I am telling my story for the first time. And those were precisely my feelings."

What effect does playback theatre have on the audience, the company, and the social context in which it is embedded? This question can be described and determined based on the criteria of the appropriateness within the social context. The aim is to integrate appropriately the individual stories, but also the entire performance, within the given social context, and in so doing to transform this context. (The main responsibility for this task rests with the conductor.) For both the third and fourth question "it-statements" can be formulated: "This performance absolutely hit the mark," or, "This story could only be told and performed in this group and this situation." In our example (in later discussions with the players): "What taboos are at work in the way we treat foreign students that we do not ask them about their experiences and are not interested in their stories? Are we capable of performing their stories on stage?"

The resulting chart of research questions about the effectiveness of playback theatre appears opposite.

In short, it is indisputable for practitioners of playback *that* playback theatre 'works' in various dimensions. However, in order to describe scientifically this effectiveness and to be able to mutually verify it in the context of practical research, we require a way to speak about various perspectives, criteria, and styles. What sorts of benefits in knowledge are hoped for in the practice of playback theatre through such research?

Avenues for Research

The following discussion is explicitly *not* about a broad presentation of various stage-forms, applications, or special techniques in playback theatre. (Some of these questions are discussed in other contributions to this volume.) Instead, the following reflections are limited to formulating *one* possible research question of particular interest for playback for each of these four dimensions (as well as their connections to one another). These questions will be examined by means of a hypothesis within each of the

Content Dimension	Artistic Dimension
criterion: Congruence (authentic interpretation)	*criterion*: Staging (appropriate representation)
question: How is playback 'effective' from the teller's viewpoint?	*question:* What makes a performance effective?
Is the story authentic? Which overt and covert themes will be taken up and transformed?	Is the portrayal of the story appropriate? Does it correspond to the main theme and various aspects?
aim: Personal meaningfulness	*aim*: Artistic form

Ritualistic Dimension	Social Dimension
criterion: Understanding (deep cultural hermeneutics)	**criterion:** Interaction (systemic fitting together)
question: What does playback theatre 'achieve' and how does it 'work' from the perspective of the interaction between teller, conductor, players and audience? Does the story and its adaptation deepen mutual understanding? How is the 'connecting thread' tied in?	**question:** What 'consequences' does playback theatre have on the social context in which it is embedded? Does the performance on the whole fit the social context? Does it transform the context?
aim: Collective meaningfulness	*aim:* Social integration

various dimensions and/or perspectives and illustrated with examples.

From the **individually subjective perspective**, playback theatre 'works' because the story verbally reported by the storyteller is not just told, but also reembodied through movement, words, dialogue, voice, and music (as well as supported by the entire scene).

If the stories playing a central role in playback theatre were only told or recited and then were talked about, they would not reach this point of immediate recognition, which often takes place in playback. This recognition is often combined with the subjective feeling of being truly understood and receiving a gift through the play. The performance of a written play can also trigger emotion and consternation. This was the goal of the Greek tragedies. However, these seldom resulted in the experience typical for playback theatre, in which one's own truth is encountered in an encompassing, perhaps even broadened sense.

I suspect that this is the point at which Fox actually connects to the tradition of preliterary theatre. Orally told and spontaneously played stories undermine the separation of thinking and acting to which we are all conditioned by growing up in a civilization of written culture:

> The separation of thinking and acting finds a correlation in perception. Writing transforms the sound of oral speech into spatial symbols, which can be visually perceived. This favors the dominance of the visual in the occidental development over all other senses. This cultural hierarchy of bodily senses and their neurophysical processing leads to a behavior of distance, which also makes it psychologically possible to separate the constitution of the individual from its environment. To the extent to which vocal literacy and writing asserted itself as the dominant medium of communication, the culture and humankind, with its psychophysical as well as mental capacities, developed the aforementioned strategies. The Western theatre as a part of this culture supported this process.[9]

Not without reason, this aspect gains great importance in the training of playback troupes. What is practiced is not the dramatic translation of a text from abstract symbols into a literal body, but rather the spontaneous expression of unconsciously stored moving images.

The manner in which the conductor opens and leads the interview is decisive for an authentic interpretation of the story. In the process, the conductor aims to make the essence of the story clear for both the players and the audience. Most importantly the storyteller must be able to recognize his or her own themes in the artistically condensed version. Many general questions can be asked at this point, about such matters as the meaning of language and the personality of the storyteller.

A specific question for research could be, According to which "rules" should the interview be conducted? Or to what extent does the interview in playback theatre differ from other therapeutic, biographical, or journalistic forms of interviewing?

*From the **collectively subjective perspective** playback theatre 'works' because the storytelling is not limited to a personal meaning, but rather creates a collective meaning of a contingent reality.[10] The personal meaning of the story lies in the dialectical crossing over of the individual stories that are told with those that remain untold. Almost always, the stories answer each other in a highly complex form.*

Example: Towards the end of a twelve-day experiential training session, two groups were formed, each of which prepared a performance for the other. In the morning performance by the first group, the storytellers came from the second group. The four stories dealt with the following themes: Where do I root myself? What must I leave behind? Which life do I choose? What have I lost, personally, culturally, and politically? What else is there? What new freedoms have I gained? What is the price of this freedom?

In the afternoon performance by the second group, the storytellers came from the first group. Their three stories focused on, What can I (trust myself to) handle? How do I deal with unforeseen challenges? How do I take the difficult first step? How can I be, and remain, ready to do the right thing at the right time in order not to be overrun?

Not only did the first story in the morning (saying goodbye to a loved city) correspond to the last in the afternoon (saying goodbye to a loved relationship). In addition, on the group level, the themes of the stories and experiences in the afternoon reflected those they had played and/or conducted in the morning, such as dealing with new challenges.

One day later, the final story of the workshop was told and enacted—a dream about career prospects and recognition from authorities. The story was played twice, first as it was dreamt and thereafter as what the storyteller hoped for (the transformed version). His last comment was: "What is important for me is to see that in the second version, I was given the responsibility and had the freedom to do what I wanted." This last workshop story provided an answer to the entire group process as well as to individual stories from individual storytellers.

The sociologist and philosopher Hannah Arendt writes in her portrait of raconteuse Isak Dinesen: "It is true that storytelling reveals meaning without committing the error of defining it, that it brings about consent and reconciliation with things as they really are, and that we may even trust it to contain eventually by implication that last word which we expect from the 'day of judgement'." [11] Therefore, on an unconscious level, stories can be linked via a connecting thread. They can even transform one another. In this manner the beginning and end of a performance are often connected. A number of spatial and social rituals that are practiced in playback theatre, such as "Let's watch," serve to bring all participants into a less consciously controlled, while at the same time broadened, state of awareness.

However, without this ritualized framework—of a beginning and end of a performance, of the invitation and the bidding farewell to the storyteller after the portrayal of the story—this connecting thread cannot develop. Instead the risk arises that the performance may decline into general confusion. As a principle gained through experience, one can assume that the players perform more creatively and freely, as they feel secure and supported in the ritual created by the conductor throughout the performance. Thus, the research question arises: *How does the ritual in playback theatre differ from the rituals of other forms of theatre and other rituals in cults, religions, and political contexts?*

From the **individually objective perspective**, playback theatre 'works' when the players successfully integrate the conscious and unconscious, individual and collective, main and sub-themes of a story and convert them into appropriate and artistic moving 'images'.

As practitioners of playback theatre know, this capacity is based on a spontaneity related to a shamanic state of awareness and only developed after years of training. This difficult-to-describe state of awareness emerges from the interplay between excitement and inner emptiness, in the sense of empty vessel, which makes a particular kind of artistic spontaneity possible.

Fox writes on this subject:

Spontaneity first requires that the senses be open to information from the environment. To accomplish this receptor task, we must be in the moment, animal-like. Second, we must be able to stand outside the moment to make sense of what is occurring. We can then take action—that is, perform a conscious act—which is no small achievement. This action will in turn create a new environmental condition. Thus, spontaneity is the ability to maintain a free-flowing constantly self-adjusting cycle of sensory input, evaluation, and action.[12]

This state of consciousness, also known as the "middle modus of awareness,"[13] is, as far as I know, the subject of little scientific research. However, it is characteristic for all kinds of artists. Apparently, this state arises from a melding of partly individual and partly archetypal-collective 'images' on two levels—from basic feelings and basic archetypal pictures. Very clearly this is not about the conscious translation of semantic meaning into symbolic forms of expression, but rather about a kind of creative emptiness (or trance consciousness), which similar to dreams, is rooted in a deeper level of the systematic nature of the human mind.[14]

The following research questions arise, among others: *How can this state of consciousness be more closely described? How does it differ from other forms of artistic spontaneity? How can the essence of a story be grasped and expressed? How can the untold and yet tangible elements of a story, the invisible half, be portrayed? What forms are appropriate?*

From the **collectively objective perspective**, *playback theatre 'works' through a 'connecting pattern' between the story, the portrayal, and the social context of the performance, which is more in keeping with a yogic culture than western customs.*[15]

In occidental theatre performances the context plays a minor role, beginning with who buys a ticket. Nevertheless the performance itself is usually not affected by this context.[16] From the beginnings of playback theatre, there lay a new connection between spontaneity and service to the community. I presume that this concept has something to do with Fox's experience as a member of the American Peace Corps in Nepal. The Western theatre lies in a tradition that was greatly influenced by morality and enlightenment. Nevertheless, modern theatre directors, in contrast to the conductor of a playback performance, do not view "service to the community" as part of their work. Whether or not the "pattern that connects" develops at all is largely dependent on the sensitivity and artistic skills of the conductor. This is less about "creating" the context than expressing the trust that everything necessary for a good performance is there; that this performance here-and-now is unique and can never be repeated; that the direction is open-ended. The real and the spiritual space in which the conductor, storyteller, players, and audience find themselves does not separate them, but rather connects them. This is increasingly the case—the more successfully a performance gives room to different positions and perspectives, creating new relations among the participants. This is no doubt enhanced when players represent different ages and life experiences.

Whether or not this connecting indeed happens is not subject to some quasi-natural law, but rather is an event arising out of the voluntary decision of all. Nevertheless it is not automatic.[17]

Out of this research questions arise, including: *What are the conditions which support this happening? Why and how is it sometimes successful and other times not? In which contexts—professional, educational, and political—is playback theatre possible? To what extent is a performance influenced by such a context? Could and should the context be explicitly referred to, perhaps even brought on stage? Can playback theatre deepen the relationships within a community, or perhaps even create a new community? In particular, is playback theatre a "technique" that is applicable independent of context, or does its effectiveness elude any attempt to implement it towards a particular aim? What kind of experience is gained through the interplay of the various dimensions in playback theatre—content, ritual, artistic form, and social interaction?*

Mystery and Play

Depending on the fundamental meta-theory various answers are possible. From the perspective of depth psychology, Laurens van der Post writes, in the tradition of C.G. Jung:

> There is... a kind of experience, in which recognition lies simultaneously above and below the level of consciousness. There is a way through which the collective knowledge of humanity expresses itself individually in mere daily life so that life itself becomes pure knowledge. In any event, for me this is life: a mystery in every form of its being, a restless, perfect mystery."[18]

However, can the mystery of life be researched?

From the perspective of social science, this question of practical intention can only be clarified through a pluralistic *discourse about various worlds*, which as human beings we belong to simultaneously and for periods of time: the material world of *objectivity*, the social world of *shared subjectivity*, and the personal world of *subjectivity*.

Adjoining Habermas's theory of communicative action, playback theatre can be understood as a form of communicative, "educative" theatre, which renders an authentic, public sphere for critical discourse, in which storytelling and aesthetic forms of knowledge find a new space. Here, instead of dependence on experts, the daily experiences and stories of members of a community are heard and respected, and the creativity and emancipated potential buried by our schools and universities can be rediscovered and revitalized.[19]

The well-known Bohemian Bishop Johann Amos Comenius, precursor and forerunner to education of the enlightenment period, made a suggestion in his widely forgotten *Schola Ludus* [School as Play]. He wrote to the schoolmaster at the founding of a "praiseworthy school in Patak" in the year 1654:

> Finally, people's lives (particularly those who will serve in churches, governments and schools, and those are the kinds of people that schools take on to educate) thrive on speaking and acting—in this manner the youth will be led through example and emulation without complaint or waste of time to respect the differences in backgrounds and the differences depending on the given situation; to take on the appropriate gesticulation and composure, with the face, hands and entire body; to express the feelings of the moment; to change the voice and to switch with a word; to play each role with respect; and with all this to free oneself from an almost peasant-like awkwardness.[20]

What Comenius recommended for the individual and societal education of future theologians, educators and legal representatives—acting in school and school as play—is fundamentally valid for our day. For both the players and the audience, there hardly exists a more effective and entertaining framework for examining individual and collective relations as this structure of a "mirror-theatre" [21] resurrected to a public stage.

Comenius wanted to employ theatre in school in order to prepare future civil servants (in the church, government, and education) for their work in a still widely class-structured society.[22] In contrast, modern playback theatre creates a ritual framework in which an open society can confront itself with its own multifaceted reflection. Viewed as such, the above outline of questions formulated for researching the practice of playback theatre could develop a new focus for critical research in social science and the study of education.

Notes

[1] Translated from German by the author.

[2] Laurens van der Post, *Das dunkle Auge Afrikas* (Berlin: Henssel, 1956), 85f.

[3] Jonathan Fox, *Acts of Service: Spontaneity, Commitment, Tradition in the Nonscripted Theatre* (New Paltz, NY: Tusitala Publishing, 1994), 198.

[4] Jo Salas, *Improvising Real Life: Personal Story in Playback Theatre* (New Paltz, NY: Tusitala, 1993).

[5] Fox, *Acts of Service*, 216.

[6] Currently in Germany, various institutions are considering implementing trial programs in technical colleges, teaching colleges, and universities in Hannover, Freiburg and Kassel.

[7] "How does playback theatre work?" is an Anglo-Saxon formulation of the problem; the Teutonic formulation would be, "Upon what epistemology does playback base itself?" The Japanese would presumably ask, "Who were the teachers of Jonathan Fox and Jo Salas?" Compare to Johan Galtung, "Structure, culture and intellectual style: an essay comparing Saxonic, Teutonic, Gallic and Nipponic approaches," in *Social Science Information* (London and Beverly Hills: Sage, 1981), 817-856.

[8] I am fully aware that the following argument is based on a social science research paradigm that is familiar to *me* and therefore close at hand. There are certainly other just as valid approaches to speaking about the effectiveness of playback theatre. When in the following paper the term effectiveness, or something similar, is used, in no way is a linear cause-and-effect correlation meant.

[9] Lambert Blum, "'Unterwerfung des Theaters unter das Wort': Theater als literarisiertes Medium," in *Tragt Masken. Schont das eigene Gesicht*, Johannes Beck, Jörg Holkenbrink & Anne Kehl, eds. (Bremen: Institut für Kulturforschung und Bildung, Bremen University, Edition Temmen, 1996), 150.

[10] "Stories are told and every story has a beginning and end. The telling of stories 'reconciles' with reality not only like understanding, in which the contingent reality is

lent meaning, but rather through the simple fact that there is a set end, it provides that the principle of a beginning is made conscious." See Ursula Ludz's introduction to Hannah Arendt, *Ich will verstehen* (Munich Piper, 1996), 23.

[11] Hannah Arendt, "Isak Dinesen 1885-1963," in *Men in Dark Times* (New York: Harcourt, Brace and World, 1968), 105.

[12] Fox, *Acts of Service*, 101.

[13] "The self is spontaneous, in the middle modus... rather the unity before and after the separation of activity and passivity, which includes both." See Frederick S. Perls, Ralph Hefferline & Paul Goodman, eds., *Gestalt-Therapy* (New York: Academic Press, 1951), 164.

[14] See Gregory Bateson, *Ecology of Mind* (New York: Ballantine, 1972), 128-153.

[15] Yogic culture does not know the strict separation between presence, past, and future, art and science, theatre and life, audience and players, as is common in the West.

Gregory Bateson writes about this, "As I see it, the world consists out of a complex network... The reward of such work is not power, but rather beauty." (Bateson, *Ecology of Mind*, 268-269).

[16] Naturally, this is not valid for the wide tradition of politically active theatre of this century from Bertolt Brecht to Augusto Boal and Dario Fo, who for their part drew from the old forms of Commedia dell'Arte.

[17] Because of this, social scientists performing practical research can only utilize forms of participants' observations.

[18] Laurens van der Post, *Vorstoss ins Innere, Afrika und die Seele des XX Jahrhunderts* (Berlin: Henssel, 1960), 163.

[19] See Anne Berkeley, "Forming Critical Spaces: Habermas, Theatre Pedagogy, and the Public Sphere," unpublished article, Department of Theatre, University of Maryland, College Park, MD, n.d.

[20] Johann Amos Comenius, "*Schola Ludus d.i. Die Schule als Spiel*," in H. Beyers, *Bibliothek paedogogischer Klassiker* (Langensalza, 1888), 4f.

[21] The playback theatre group led by Marlies Arping and Daniel Feldhendler in Frankfurt/Main call themselves "Spiegelbühne Frankfurt" or "Mirror-stage Frankfurt."

[22] Civil servants of churches, schools, and legal representatives of the past are now joined by therapists as the guarantors of the societal order. Are they fascinated by playback theatre because it allows role switching on stage in Comenius's sense of education?

LAYERS OF MEANING
Research and Playback Theatre—A Soulful Construct

Tarquam McKenna

Research traditionally has been viewed as a search for data, something presented externally to be observed and experimented on, with an external locus of control. Playback attends to interiority, the inner world, and the data are the experiences of the audiences and actors. In this sense it is different from experimental research which "tests" ideas. When one is researching into playback theatre there is a need not only to perceive the surface of the memoirs, to watch the performance, but to bear witness to their 'soul'. Ethnographers faced this problem in seeking to understand the meanings of foreign tribes, but they let the truth reside in an interpretation of meanings. Here we are trying to reach an understanding of other persons, of stories embodied in the external rituals of stage. How can we carry out this research without recourse to the superficial? How can it be revealed to us?

The purpose of this paper is to see to what extent the observational research paradigms of ethnography, analysis of biography, and heuristics can apply or be adapted to playback theatre. It is also to examine to what extent the analysis or construction of theory can relate experiences so immediate and contextually contingent to something which appears to be transcendental, numinous, and essential. My thesis is to argue that playback theatre can be used to construct a sense of purposeful engagement and is a way to develop an 'essential understanding of the self,' by moving beyond a mere 'functional' notion of identity. I hope also to illustrate that there is a relationship between interiority and artistry, and that ultimately playback theatre can be seen as a soul-making tool. This paper is a yearning for the deep stories, the intangible accounts of understanding, that move beyond the philosophical, psychological, and aesthetic experience to the realm of the numinous. The emergence of a scientistic model of inquiry in arts therapies has enabled a strengthening of the value (validity) of art as a means (instrument) to wholeness (outcomes).

A Return to Soul

This chapter builds on my earlier academic writings in which I have written of the need for research that considered the 'soul'. This call for the return to soul, which I hold is central to the identity of playback theatre, continues in this paper. If many of us have been robbed of our true biography, then playback theatre is *a* way to remember the dismembering.[1] It brings biography, intimacy and soulfulness together. Playback provides us with a way to wholeness and soul must be seen as the seminal notion in the identity of this theatre art form. As Plotinus says, from the soul all things begin. Carl Gustav Carus, the German court physician (1789-1869), wrote that understanding comes when "those wonderful and mysterious processes of the unconscious world of the soul are understood by the conscious mind; if it sees itself supported by the unconscious like a rainbow floating lightly over a dark wall of rain clouds, then the basis of essential understanding is at hand..." [2]

Playback Theatre has moments when it attends to collectivity, identity, and ritual, using theatre as a way to life-making. The stories in playback are often the soul-journeys towards the "numinous" realm that hold the teller in their truths.

I invite the reader to consider the well-made playback performance as a 'memoir'.[3] The actors, musicians, and conductors become a mirror for the teller, who has a need for the story to be told. The playback performance brings the audience and actors to a place where their 'search for grand narratives' will be enmeshed with personal stories or 'more local, small scale theories' which are 'tales of the field.' [4]

Dismembering

The experience for the teller of the enactment in playback is not only a retelling, but also an occasion of deeper and fuller knowing. It may be that there is a different consciousness 'raising' as a consequence of the art form. Playback theatre is always a ritualistic occasion. In this theatre form a human being attends to his or her self and at times to something greater than the self. In this respect I have written elsewhere of the 'journey' or 'quest'.[5] Playback theatre can become a metaphorical quest for meaning. In educational, psychotherapeutic, social, and community contexts playback theatre is engaged as a means of collaboration for entering multiple realities, which can include those beyond the *habitus* of daily life. Playback demands a disciplined approach to artistry, which brings a shaking of our roots, where the action is like a conversation leading to conversion to another way of being, behaving, and gnosis.[6] Playbackers call the occasion of shaking of our roots "deep stories."

The telling of the story (conversation) is the first stage of awareness, as the story is told to two audiences, the actors and the theatre audience. It is an active telling, not the passive presentation of scientific objects of research. To see our lives mirrored in the re-actions of others is a re-re-presentation, which is both privately and publicly reflexive (for teller and theatre audience respectively). The teller yearns for wholeness (conversion) and the playback form is *one* unique representation of this call to wholeness. It is in the seeing of the re-enactment that there is a strengthening in the move towards wholeness. The art form of playback theatre for some tellers becomes an occasion for the 'fitting together' of lost pieces. In the following table I have stressed that that which is crucial to playback theatre is a teller's awareness of the audience to whom she feels compelled to tell her story (table 1). As the teller enters into the telling in a confessional or 'deep storied' manner, then she requires an audience to witness. In witnessing the story, the move towards integration occurs.

The conversation metaphor does not assume that we can only construct the idea of a self in relation to the reactions of other social beings. Playback is a way of revealing beyond mere re-constructing. Conversation also implies intentionality on the part of all participants, and this is one of the things that makes playback theatre so different from empirical research—not just playback's search for meanings, but also the purposeful

TABLE 1 **A PLACE FOR PLAYBACK AS A RESEARCH INSTRUMENT** [7]				
Research Perspective	**Experimental**	**Naturalistic**	**Transformative**	**Playback Theatre**
Focus	Comprehension	Interpretation	Learning	Liberation
Vehicle	Prediction	Description	Collaboration	Connectivity
Intent	Add Credence	Uncover Theories of Meaning	Interrogate Assumptions & Beliefs	Breaking Silences to Know our Truths
Researcher's Stance	I Priorities	I-You Invisible Invisible	We Vulnerable	Us Service with Dignity
Stance on Knowledge	Fixed	Contextual	Relational	Co-creational
Procedure	Test Hypothesis	Multiple Perspectives	Tensions & Anomalies	Movement toward Integration
Methodological Stance	Innocent	Relative	Democratic	Transformational
Path to Understanding	Simplicity	Complexity	Reflexivity	Inter-Reflexivity (Public) Intra-Reflexivity (Private)
Role of Research Relative to Schooling in Our Society	Cultural Literacy	Cultural Diversity	Morality	Soulful and Emotional Literacy
How Significance Determined	Individual	Cooperative	Collaborative	Witnessing **is** connectivity through intimacy
Results	Better or Cleaner Arguments	More Complex Explanations	Learning & New Invitation to Inquiry	Invitations to 'Entrancement' and communion
Presentational Form	Report	Story	Invitation	Aesthetic Theatre
Product	Study	Thick Description	Journey	Soulful Understanding

and shared revelations of meanings.

In the immediacy of the performance teller, actors, and audience are all invited to see their individual and collective lives from a new perspective. Sometimes this conversion brings a total shift, as the self is confronted; other times a softer, gentler transformation occurs, as the self undergoes a subtle metamorphosis. In all instances participants are enticed to a new way of seeing, behaving, and knowing. However, it is the seeing *beyond* the habitus that interests me as a teacher, researcher, and playback conductor.

Most current contextual research dynamics exclude intimacy as a way of knowing. This is a quality of humanness that is challenging to define. Emotional valencies expressed in artforms are frequently of necessity "bracketed" off for empirical researchers, since these are regarded as mere epiphenomena and intangible.[8] The endeavor to apply some systematic analysis to knowing does occur in research. Analysis is not inappropriate. However I suggest most research is too heavily concerned with logos only, with little attention to eros. Soulfulness is of necessity holistic and perceptually defined. Playback theatre is inconclusive and generative and therefore is doomed to failure when tested by experimental, naturalistic and transformative modes of inquiry as given in table 1. (Experimental research, as mentioned earlier, involves the testing of hypotheses building on axioms of meaning; naturalistic research draws on a natural setting to "hear" the experiences of the researched group; and transformational research aims to not only know meaning through hypotheses and the natural experiences of the researched group, but ultimately to bring change to that community.)

Playback offers occasions to develop multiple meanings, the opening up of wider or new horizons, so different from the scientific "seizing the one correct representation" which fits the theory. Playback is able to move beyond the known horizons to a place where there are other aspects of truth, a holistic place which gives us as tellers and audience other ways of looking at ourselves.

Given this discussion, questions arise which warrant further examination: Are playback theatre practitioners concerned with the potency of the imperceptible world and the inner culture of people? Does playback theatre cosmology embrace a strong correspondence between the macrocosm and the microcosm? Does it embrace "quality praxis," including all dimensions of phenomenal reality? In playback theatre is both the macrocosm and microcosm lived out through creative endeavor, thereby enabling the community of audience and actors alike to reflect on a variety of models to interpret their individual and collective 'consciousness' beyond the mundane? Does playback offer a quest for wholeness whilst not precluding social concerns? In playback theatre are we asked to look at areas of life that are complex central institutions of inner-world views alongside the macro-sociological views? Can playback attend to the manner in which we confer meaning that is expressive of the foundations or *raison d'être* of our inner (micro-sociological) life?

I hold that the playback actor, conductor, and community can be fully occupied with the present focus, and can at the same time, with sensitive performing, acknowledge the ancestral roots of our contemporary practice. The forms in playback theatre fulfil a bonding function that attends to the members of the audience and the actors alike. Actions within the performance can be either reinforcing of accomplishments for teller and audience, or a reframing of "failure," or parts of life that may still be unknown in the teller's mind. Playback theatre as a voice can be a place for new beginnings or a reflection on memories of the past.

Playback Theatre as an Emerging Research Method

If we engage in playback theatre and accept the soulful manner of this theatre form, then we can say that this theatre can be a truly unifying experience. I propose that our own models of research with playback and other theatre modes must now begin to reflect an awareness that addresses everything in the performance as a manifestation of an underlying process. The entire web of relationships and processes in the playback space is therefore intrinsically dynamic. Playbackers have ascribed what we believe we are doing in playback. Now we must find a way of showing that this is what we really *are* undertaking. In this proposed model of inquiry I posit that the Western metaphor of knowledge as a building block be replaced by the network of interrelatedness. One is taken to a place of expanded consciousness where movement, voice, and art interweave. In playback, both the actors and audience are entering into symbolic processes to receive and represent calls to wholeness. In playback theatre shifts in awareness, active involvement, and social reconstruction are all attended to. In this theatre form a community of memories is created where audiences are meeting together, becoming socially interdependent, participating in a ritual of discussion and decision-making, and sharing the practice of playback theatre as a way of defining their history with attention to the past and the future. Two scholars, Jerome Harste and Caroline Burke, have given a template that addresses what they call experimental, naturalistic, and transformative research.[9] Playback theatre could be viewed as a fuller and richer research perspective to these now familiar modes of understanding. The Playback Theatre Model builds a depth that is lacking in the other modes of inquiry prescribed by Harste and Burke. Playback transcends all three modes of inquiry. It does not have to accommodate them, or "go through" them, but rather offers a fuller way of knowing.

It would not be enough to see playback only as a way to know what researchers call cultural literacy or cultural diversity. Playback moves the audience and actors to places of deeper knowing or 'gnosis' that are transcendent to the word or the action. The audience and the teller are taken to a place of union within themselves. This self-fulfillment occurs because the intimate, numinous, and aesthetic come together in this art form.

In table 1, the left column represents the focus of research, the vehicle and intention of research, and the stance of knowledge to which the researcher adheres. Also illustrated are the procedures and paths to understanding embodied in the thinking of the researcher. Listed are the significance, result and presentation form of the research. Finally, the product is defined.

In adding playback theatre as a liberatory art form, the theme of connectivity becomes central. There is a shared responsibility to use theatre to know shared meanings and as such the theatre form is co-creational research. Playback is tentative by nature and the procedures inside the performance bring the actors and audience to a place of integration, where there is some shift in awareness, or transformation.

From table 1 it can be seen that with playback theatre we have an indirect, culturally constituted medium through which this private distress can be viewed or voiced, acknowledged, and potentially transformed, enabling the playback actors to use playback theatre as an art form to re-constitute their worlds and the worlds of their tellers and audiences.[10] An intrapsychic reconstitution or transformation occurs for the teller and the audience through deepening the level of accessibility to unconscious materials transcending the ordinary sense of self. I have engaged Jo Salas's notion of "entrancement" to consider one outcome of playback as a research instrument.[11] Western consciousness is too heavily centered on a rationalizing, abstracting, and controlling ego. Frequently the individual no longer has the ability to perceive other realities. Here playback theatre is being used as 'gestures of soul'. These gestures of soul are the call to emotional literacy and beyond to moments where there is a sense of ultimacy and consequently soulful literacy.[12] The path to understanding for the individual is both a private (intra-reflexive) and public (inter-reflexive) process. Indigenous cultures have always had a special, codified, and ritualized awareness of the Self, the archetype of wholeness and the regulating center of the personality that transcends the ego. Transcendence in the playback theatre performance results in a 'communion' or a quality of mutual relatedness based on a co-created relationship through aesthetically rich theatre.

The broad concerns and limitations of research in theatre and drama have been noted above. Table 1 indicates how playback theatre builds on the model of artistry alluded to earlier. I now want to propose that playback theatre is in itself a reliable research instrument if we use the lens of heuristics and ethnography to explore its inner validity. Playback theatre allows for the emergence of relevant concepts discovered during the course of conducting performances and additionally enables observation of a wide range of phenomena. It could be seen as a research instrument that is generative and allows innumerable relationships to be explored.

Playback Theatre as a Journey into Entrancement and Communion

The metaphor of the journey is affirmed in Harste and Burke's paradigm for transformative research. In playback theatre the journey and the descriptions of the journey through enactment are always seen as partial truths, since the mode of communication used is always incomplete, as culture itself is incomplete. We are reminded that culture itself is not precisely boundaried and continually evolves.[13] In this sense playback theatre replicates the metaphors and symbols of a culture. The teller, conductor, and company of actors recreate an incomplete, imprecisely boundaried picture, and the playback performance is a reflection, or mirror, of the teller's field of inquiry. In the telling and re-telling of the story a continual transformation occurs. It is as close as we can get to recreation of the world of the teller with attention to his or her interiority. This seems to be the goal of play-back theatre.

Playback Theatre as a Journey into Soulful and Emotional Literacy

The emphasis of research within the field of playback theatre must be a multi-modal construction of the "nature of reality," attending to an "intimate relationship" between the teller, conductor, and the audience community.[14] This method will seek to bring the teller's phenomenological experiences to the occasion of playback theatre so that these experiences will become a performance, which is an emic or insider's view of consciousness. The teller's intimacies are seen within the performance. The intimacy of performance will lead to an understanding of the inner world of the teller. Strong playback theatre pays a great deal of attention to the art making and the rituals that support the audience and actors in their emerging views of narrative and consciousness.

> The conductor is variously a listener and a filter of the teller's meanings that the actors translate into performance. The manner of hearing which the conductor embodies is not unlike a priest or therapist.[15] The confessional quality of conversation might be similar, but this must always be without moralistic judgement. Tellers are always in charge of their telling. The conductor hears the tale and thereby invites the first disclosure of the meaning that the teller has. In speaking of the conductor as therapist, there is an assumption that may need clarification. The conductor is *like* a therapist, but unlike the therapist does not have a goal of healing. The conductor and the teller are both in an ambiguous space of hearing and reframing the tale. This does not assume the conductor 'knows' the story (or a pathology) of the teller. In this respect, there is less therapist and more witness, as the conductor is mediating between both the teller and actors alike. The word "conduit" has been employed in Perth as a way of describing the conductor's role. The conduit notion implies that the task of the conductor is to mediate in order to create a flow of rich, unimpeded, and smooth meaning.[16]

Playback Theatre as an Artful Reflexive Methodology

Playback Theatre provides us with a framework, a reflexive methodology, which demands that the narratives and the performance be seen not only as spoken, but moved texts. It is clear that the nature of well-made playback theatre demands that tellers be in charge of their stories. They rite their way into consciousness by telling and retelling their tales of the field. The actors and conductors are the colors from which the teller creates the richest picture. Tellers write their autobiography with attention to the silences, shapes, and aesthetics of who they are.

Playback Theatre as a Journey Acknowledging Connectivity

Playback as a way to autobiography affirms the importance of spontaneity, intuition, and creativity. The strength of autobiography is becoming more apparent as researchers employ this mode of inquiry more frequently. Louise Smith writes of biographical methods. Reflecting on her own experiences in qualitative research, she suggests that the autobiography became "the most important experience in my life," a "turning point." She considers that autobiography is one of the most rapidly developing and, recently, one of the most controversial forms of research. "Autobiography suggests the power of agency in social and literary affairs... It usually, but not always, eulogizes the subjective, the important part of human existence, over the objective." [17] This is another essential reason to include autobiography as a way of recollecting within the framework of playback theatre. Playback theatre is by its very nature autobiographical. It is writing your own and often a new story with the attention of the audience. The audience serves as witness to what the teller is becoming in a profoundly intimate manner.

Playback theatre closely correlates with heuristics, as it demands the in-dwelling of questions so that answers arise spontaneously and creatively. The emphasis on self-disclosure requires an immersion that is self-searching. The acquisition of personal and public information is created and adds to what is known in the researcher's mind. In playback theatre the narrator or teller is always in the teller's chair to spontaneously witness the intuitive and creative interplay. The realization phase in the action itself is the synthesis which brings a fuller dimension of understanding to audience and teller.[18] The teller in this instance may have her epiphany at the moment of performance, or after the event. The ultimate purpose of the performance is to cast light on a focused problem or theme by living through a series of questions internally. It is the teller's task to address sources of being and non-being as the stories are witnessed in their playback. It is the actors' task to perform from hunches, ideas, and essences as they emerge.

The quality of decisions that will be made in the playback theatre performance is constituted by ambiguity, excitement, and agony and requires the development of a metacognition which is not built only on factual weight or the theoretical places being created, but rather brings a narrative strength based on rhetorical devices, convincing the audience that this is another person's way of being. Playback theatre brings the community of witnesses mentioned above to a place where the performance is seen as being totally alive. This aliveness may be a reflection on the past or a moment of insight about the future. Playback theatre requires that the actor and audience as participant observers undergo a 'living through' of the concern of the hosting culture (the teller) created inside the performance contract.

We are obliged to consider the art works created in playback theatre as reflections of a rich culture and the journeys of our tellers as ways into relationship with multiple layers of reality for the community of witnesses. I hope I have encouraged playback theatre practitioners to move beyond the postmodern critiques of 'documentary' through this praxis, to move beyond a mere development of a 'sociology of life' or the slice of life approach, and thereby consider playback theatre as a means of developing a series of expressions of artistic and soulful engagements.

The quality of relatedness that I have alluded to in this essay requires that we move to a place where we can inquire of playback theatre with attention to the depth of interiority, where imagination, mystery, art, poetry, music, and intuition are equally valued. The attention to the deep stories is unique to our research and critiquing of playback theatre. Deep stories are unique to the art form of playback theatre and are central to its identity. The recognizing of the aesthetic realm which "analyzes" truths or "comprehends" from gesture and tone *is more* holistic than a mere scientific propositional mode of knowing. Playback theatre is a soulful place where there is a yearning for transcendence alongside a sense of reverence for the mysteries of the performance and the process of art-making.

Let us not forget the call to soul as unsuspected realities and unknown worlds open up before us through this art.

References

Arnold, R. "Drama, Psychodynamics and English Education." *English in Australia* 108 (June 1994): 17-27.

Carroll, J. "Video Lives: Dramatic Role and Emotional Literacy." Paper presented at 2nd World Congress of Drama/Theatre and Education, Brisbane, 1995.

Conti, G., J.E. Counter & L.C. Paul. "Transforming as Community through Research." *Convergence XXIV* 3 (1991).

Cousineau, P., ed. *Soul—An Archaeology.* London: Thorsons, 1995.

Denzin, N.K. & Y.S. Lincoln, eds. *Handbook of Qualitative Research.* Thousand Oaks, CA: Sage, 1994.

Douglass, B. & C. Moustakas. "Heuristic Inquiry: The Internal Search to Know." *Journal of Humanistic Psychology* (25) 3 (1985): 39-55.

Grainger, R. *The Glass of Heaven: The Faith of the Dramatherapist.* London: Jessica Kingsley, 1995.

Hillman, J. *The Soul's Code: In Search of Character And Calling.* New York: Random House, 1996.

McKenna, T. "Playback Theatre and Behaviour Management," *WA Teachers Journal,* November (1992).

_____. "Transformational Research and Drama Education." In *Educational Drama.* W. Michaels, ed. Sydney: NSW Education Department, 1993.

_____. "Using Playback Theatre and Behaviour Management in Schools." *Behaviour Problems Network Newsletter,* No. 15 (1993).

_____. *Playback Theatre in Action.* With Robyn Bett. Department of Language Arts Education, Edith Cowan University, video, 1993.

_____. "Drama Research Must Have Soul." *National Association for Drama in Education* 18, No. 2 (1994).

_____. "Speaking Strictly–Language is More Than Words." *Teacher Monthly,* Hangzhou P.R.C. Jiaoxue Yuekan (China Education Journal), No. 9 (1995): 32-34.

Miller, H. *The Wisdom of the Heart.* New York: New Directions, 1960.

Ruddell, R., M. R. Ruddell, & H. Singer, eds. *Theoretical Models of Process in Reading.* Newark, DE: International Reading Association, 1994.

Scott, N.A. "Criticism and the Religious Horizon." In *Humanities, Religion and the Arts Tomorrow.* H. Hunter, ed. New York: Holt, Rinehart & Winston, 1972.

Notes

1. See Hillman, *The Soul's Code*.

2. Cited in Cousineau, *Soul—An Archeology*, 46.

3. P. Stoller, and C. Olkes, "In the Sorcery's Shadow: A Memoir of Apprenticeship Among the Songhay of Niger," in Denzin & Lincoln, *Handbook*.

4. The field is the turf from which the tales grow for the playback performance. The stories of the tellers within the playback theatre performance might fall into major styles— realistic performance, confessional performance, and impressionistic performance tales (after the work of Van Maanen). See also Y.S. Lincoln, "Notes toward a fifth generation evaluation: Lessons from the voiceless, or Toward a post modern politics of evaluation," in Denzin & Lincoln, *Handbook*.

5. T. McKenna, "Transformational Research and Drama Education," in Michaels, *Educational Drama*.

6. I believe Durkheim said this of spiritual experiences. Ritual and theatre have a social role in that they bring focus to our needs to express ideas—both profane and sacred.

7. After the work of Harste & Burke (from Conference Notes given by John Carroll).

8. As a teacher in drama in special education (1981-85), I worked with people who were severely stressed. After relaxation "training," a principal asked if perhaps I could measure the eyelid flutters or skin galvanic response to validate how relaxed the person was. I knew from my relationship with the student, developed over three years, that there were shifts in his quality of being. Defining these intangibles was my dilemma.

9. Conference Notes from John Carroll. See also "Literacy as Curricular Conversations about Knowledge, Inquiry, and Morality," in Ruddell, Ruddell & Singer, *Theoretical Models of Process in Reading*, 1233.

10. I would like to suggest that this is an area for further research. The question is to be addressed in another paper in which I would ask the question "What does a playback actor do with the self as he or she performs?" Alternatively we might ask how "open" can you be to become a community of actors that is the palette from which the teller and conductor paint the picture?

11. See Jo Salas' essay in this volume.

12. See Carroll, *Video Lives*.

13. Denzin & Lincoln, *Handbook*, 407.

14. *Handbook*, 4.

15. Grainger's text, *The Glass Of Heaven*, looks at the use of dramatherapy and seems to give a full examination of the qualities of hearing that the priest and therapist both engage in.

16. Jonathan Fox explained the conductor role in these terms when he first came to Perth. See his *Acts of Service*, 121.

17. L. Smith, in Denzin & Lincoln, *Handbook*, 288.

18. Douglass & Moustakas, "Heuristic Inquiry," 39-55.

Playback Portrait

MARIANNE TOBLER
Switzerland

Ten years ago, Marianne Tobler spoke with a small voice and hesitated to stand in front of a group. Today, she conducts playback theatre in front of sizable crowds with confidence and animation. This personal transformation is a benefit of the path Marianne has taken from audience member, to playback actor, to playback conductor, director, and trainer.

Marianne Tobler, 56, is a psychotherapist in Winterthur, Switzerland. A decade ago she attended a performance of playback theatre presented by Playback Theater Schweiz, a group out of Schaffhausen, Switzerland. Inspired by what she saw on stage, she became a teller and told a dream. The experience was "life-changing," says Marianne. A year later, she became a member of the company.

An actor for many years, by now Marianne finds herself more and more the leader. Following the recent departure of founder Annette Henne, she is the administrative director of PT Schweiz, which meets fortnightly (artistic direction is shared). She is also the director of a PT group of therapists and psychodrama trainers in Konstanz, Germany, and teaches playback in various settings: to counselors in Bulgaria at the University of Sophia, to Jungian psychodramatists, to a PT company in Köln, Germany.

She was also a facilitator during one of PT Schweiz's big corporate contracts, a special challenge, since effective leadership was the focus of the training.* In addition, Marianne also utilizes PT in her therapeutic work. With a male colleague, she runs a therapy group for couples, in which, when a couple "gets stuck in a story," the therapists act it out. The effectiveness of the playback is "really amazing," Marianne, says. "Through the enactment, we can get to the feeling level." This ap-

---

* See "A Model of Teamwork and Spontaneity" INTERPLAY, Vol. VII, #1, June 1996.

proach is especially effective, she adds, with people who cannot formulate their feelings: "Out of some stammered words we try to find the reality of the teller's story and bring it to the stage." Marianne trained her partner in the necessary playback skills.

A psychodramatist, Marianne commented that she brings playback into her psychodrama trainings as a means of maximizing access: "I use it when I feel everyone needs to tell and there isn't much time."

Is playback theatre still interesting nine years on? "Very much so," she says without hesitating. "There is so much variety," she adds. As well as her many conducting tasks, Marianne values her continuing role as an actor: "If I didn't have the opportunity to act, it wouldn't be so engaging."

When asked how PT is therapeutic, first, she makes the statement that PT is not therapy, but the outcome is therapeutic on many levels. She lists some of them: Being in a PT group is helpful for the couples who can't express themselves well. For herself, being in a healthy and healing group "feeds me." As an actor, it is therapeutic to move in and out of such a variety of roles. Finally, she talks about the benefit of having the chance to tell her own stories in playback. Even when she might not get a chance to tell, she adds, the process is therapeutic. "I might think about telling my story and maybe being a teller all week; so even if I don't tell, I've gone through a healthy process."

The Teller's Story
and Personal Growth

A psychological analysis of the
interpersonal and intrapsychic processes
making playback effective

András Zánkay

As a clinical psychologist and psychotherapist working with clients, and as the conductor of our playback theatre company, the question "Why does playback work?" seems important to think about. Jo Salas's book, *Improvising Real Life*, provides a very profound, precise, and artistic description of many different psychological processes concerning playback. So I see my task in this essay as merely adding something to it rather than trying to make a full psychological analysis. Playback theatre is a highly complex social event. This is what makes it so interesting and enjoyable.

My aim, therefore, is to shed light on two additional aspects of the impact of playback theatre on the teller and the audience. I will omit consideration of the company, although it, too, bears study.

Before continuing I would like to express my gratitude toward one of my teachers, Ferenc Mérei, my primary trainer in psychodrama. He was an outstanding person in the field of psychology in Hungary. His widespread activity in different areas of psychology had a seminal effect on the development of clinical, social, and developmental psychology in Hungary in the epoch of the "Iron Curtain," when psychology as a "bourgeois science" was suspicious and scarcely tolerated by the leaders of "the" party. At that time Hungary had very limited contact with the noncommunist world.

Mérei's spirit was close to J. L. Moreno's. Mérei was very much influenced by Moreno's thoughts. He wrote a book about sociometry that introduced Moreno's concepts to the Hungarian public and added many original ideas of his own. He was also the person who introduced psychodrama to Hungary. His students started to work with psychodrama in clinical settings and to train others. His work helped create the basis of the now promising development of psychodrama and playback movement in Hungary.

In one of his early works, *Shared Experience*, first published in 1948, Mérei describes the results of his investigations into the relationship between the group and the leader. He was interested in who is stronger—the socially effective leader or the members of a group whose social efficacy is about average. In his psychological experiments with children in kindergarten groups, he found that *the group is stronger*. The leader has to study and adapt to the habitual behaviors of the group, the rules of their games, and to follow the rituals and traditions of the group in order to achieve a leading position and be able to direct them.

As a result of his investigations and those of others reviewed by him, Mérei stated: "... the investigation has shown that in shared activities the developmental niveau of children's behavior increases... During the study of groups of children, starting from different positions, we concluded with the hypothesis *that an experience shared by others has greater power than one experienced alone. It is stronger in its emotional expression and is a special source of enjoyment."* [1]

These thoughts are very relevant for us as playback performers. When the teller tells his story before the company and the audience, the original experience is relived, but the situation now is very different from the original one. Now on the side of the teller, there are other people present, with open ears and open hearts. This can enable the teller to face and experience the situation more fully than was possible originally. In the present circumstances it is not so dangerous, not so overwhelming. It is good to know that this new, shared story can be stronger than the first and that the first can be rewritten—not in the sense of altering the story line, but putting it into another context and thereby changing its meaning for the teller.

We can perhaps also appreciate the relevance of Mérei's words in one of his other works, written together with some of his students, about the use of psychodrama: "The duplication of reality makes it possible to overcome it." [2] They also cite Anzieu and Martin: "Those who duplicate the world—with drawings and symbols, as well as with memories and words—affect their reality. With the repetition of experience, the past becomes past, and can enter into the determination of current behavior as a prior experience, without emotion-filled currents." [3]

It is obvious that the enactment of a story on the stage is a powerful duplication. These thoughts can lead our attention to the intrapsychic processes that make playback effective.

What Makes a Conductor a Conductor

As a conductor, I realized after a while that in order to understand a teller's story, I have to put it into a broader context. The different elements of the story have to be put into a proper perspective to get an idea about its meaning for the teller. My question to myself is what makes this story a story? If I were the teller, why would I choose this story?

At the beginning I did not find it easy to answer these questions. My awareness focussed on the emotional character of the events. The story was interesting, felt somehow important, had some kind of relevance for me. But these simple answers helped me to realize that a story has something to do with the dynamic aspects of personality. It is usually not conscious, but closely connected to our inner development.

Thinking about what connects us as human beings, I found the widespread urge to give meaning to our life. Our inner life force brings us forward in our development, wanting us to fulfill our potential. But as I once heard a trainer working in the field of organizational development say, "everybody wants to develop, but nobody wants to change." Changes in ourselves are not always pleasant. What makes change is a dynamic tension caused by conflicting forces connected to different values. Usually we don't enjoy the process of change very much, although we do enjoy the result of it.

What makes a story a story is partly its dynamic structure. Two or more forces are in contradiction: North against South, God against the Devil, the fight between the Good and the Bad Powers, the war of the Red and the White Roses in English history and the battle of the Reds and the Whites in the Russian Revolution, heard about so much in the childhood of my generation in Hungary, and so forth. This tension is what awakens our interest. We become involved and moved.

Fortunately our life is not full of battles and wars, but we do experience contradictions of different values almost every day. If we are able to satisfy one of our needs, a new need emerges before long, and after a time, we may be forced to act. It takes considerable time and effort to act in a proper way to satisfy our needs and to fulfill the values we appreciate. As we live our life and do what we do, we change and create ourselves by our actions. Usually we are not conscious of this process of changing. Our awareness is more connected to our identity, and the changes in us are usually more obvious for the people around us.

As a conductor I find it helpful to think that *our stories have a close connection to our personal development and center around moments of change.* At such moments, we are at the border of the old and the new. The old is characterized by the controversy of at least two conflicting values. In that phase of our development we are able to fulfill only one of them in a given time, at the cost of the other(s). We can't create a good balance between them; we can't bring them into harmony; we can't have them at once. What we experience in these situations is tension, nervousness. An effort is needed to achieve more harmony. This effort can bring us to the next phase, where these values are not in conflict anymore. On this higher level we don't have to choose between them and we are able to act in accordance with the requirements of the situation.

Let's look at some examples from our performances:
One evening G. came to the teller's chair and told a story about what happened to him in his student years. *It was the time of the Cuban crisis in the early sixties. He was a student teacher at a university in Budapest. The story began in the morning, when the radio announced that Krushchev, the leader of the Soviet Union, had refused the American demand to halt the Soviet ships bringing missiles into Cuba. The danger of the Third World War was very present.*

G., annoyed by the irresponsibility of the political leaders, came up with a practical joke on the way to the university with his best friend. They told this "secret" to some of their girl mates: "Krushchev is dead, but it is forbidden to make it public." Since the girls were carefully selected, all the students knew about it within two hours. A teacher who was an agent of the Ministry of Interior had also heard about it, and he wanted to know who created this rumor. When he appeared, the joke was no longer enjoyable. In the next couple of days G. faced fear of death. It became quite clear that if they were discovered, they would not be able to continue their studies and would suffer other consequences. Many people had disappeared in the recent decades, coming back from camps only years later, if ever. But the students didn't give them away, and after a week the teacher gave up his investigation.

G. told the story in a quite lighthearted manner, letting the joke dominate. But, just as it happened at the time, after a while it became far from a joke. For G., then and in the story, the value of expressing himself freely, on the one hand, and the value of being safe and not threatened, on the other, were in conflict. In the actual circumstances G. was not able to bring them into harmony. It seems to me that in telling his story, he needed to repeat his experience to be able to bring these two values into harmony in the present. The task of our company, then, was to show both sides of G.'s experience.

In another performance, A. told a story from her childhood. As an introduction she spoke about her desire to tell this story, explaining that she had done a lot of work on it in different therapeutic settings, but that she couldn't free herself from the burden of the experience. *It happened when she was eleven years old. She was raised by her mother ever since her father died when she was six months old. At the age of eleven, the cat gave birth to four kittens. During the night, when she was sleeping, the cat brought the kittens into her bed while she slept. She rolled over on three of the kittens, killing them. In the morning, when she woke up, she was horrified by what happened, but her mother didn't try to comfort her. On the contrary, the mother was angry at her, as if she killed the cats intentionally. Afterwards, the remaining kitten became her favorite, and she cared for it for all of its seventeen years.* To be accepted as she is, on the one hand, and being loved on the other, put her in a seemingly unsolvable conflict in that situation. It makes life very difficult if we have to choose to be ourselves or to be loved. During the enactment of the story on the stage, her father entered into the scene and expressed his love for her, and accepted and cuddled her. The teller received something she had waited for for decades.

One evening U. told a story. She was eleven years old and the story is about her friendship with her classmate, P. *They were very good friends, walking, talking, and playing together. They spent all the time with one another outside of class. P. was the best student in the class, with outstanding performance in all the subjects. U. loved P. very much. One day, U. caused some unintended pain for P.—at least this is what she thought must have happened, because P. started avoiding U., not even talking to her anymore. She even became friends with another girl. U. did not understand anything about the situation. She felt terrible and cried a lot. Once—having seen her crying—B. started to talk to U. and asked her what was wrong. When she heard about U.'s pain, B. began to console her. After that, they became good friends, and U. was not so lonely. She was more able now to accept the end of her friendship with P.*

U. was very moved at the telling of her story. But as she looked back on that time, it was clear to her that the pain was not so strong anymore. The tension had been lessened by the experience of being able to belong to someone, on the one hand, and not becoming dependent, on the other hand. The actors on the stage were able to play both ways of relating, the old and the new one. U. accepted the enactment.

My conclusion is that if a playback company is able to show the dynamics of the contravening forces of a story, it contributes to the release of the contradiction, and a step forward becomes possible. Sometimes it is not easy for the company to get in touch with this tension, because of the teller's style. How she tells the story can sometimes cover its painful aspect. It also depends on the company's capacity to bear tension. This reflects the relationships between the members of the company, since capacity to work under tension is built up in common work.

If the task is not solved properly during the enactment of a story, in my experience, the tension remains present. Usually the next story brings it back to the stage, sometimes in a maximized form, so that it can be handled properly. If we listen carefully to the story and enact it properly, it can assist the teller in finding a way to bring different values into harmony. This is what makes playback effective. It makes playback art, the main function of which is to promote the development of persons, communities, and humankind.

References

Clayton, G.M. *Effective Group Leadership*. Caulfield, Victoria: ICA Press, 1994.

Mérei, Ferenc. *Az egyuttes elmeny*. Budapest: 1947.

Salas, Jo. *Improvising Real Life: Personal Story in Playback Theatre*. New Paltz, NY: Tusitala Publishing, 1993.

Notes

[1] Mérei, F., *Tars es csoport* (Budapest: Akademiai Kiado,1989), 29.

[2] Mérei, F., et. al., *A pszichodrama Onismereti es terapias alkalmazasa* (Budapest: Akademiai Kiado, 1987), 16-17.

[3] D. Anzieu & J. Y. Martin, *La dynamique des groupes restreints* (Paris: PUF, 1976).

THE JOURNEY TO DEEP STORIES

Jonathan Fox

We come to the end of this book. It has been rewarding for me to spend this time gathering the contributions, immersing myself in the ideas, and letting my own playback experience be informed by the conversation. Particularly compelling for me has been the dialogue about the playback stage as a place for the deepest stories, stories that hold whole worlds of history, pain, and revelation.

This is where I have come to. When I began with playback, my dream was to perform in a New York theatre and be written up favorably by the critics. My orientation was primarily artistic, my goal to create performances rich in their composition of image, texture, energy, and sound. But from the start I also felt drawn to deep stories, at the time no more than a kind of vague possibility, almost like a mirage. If we could reach that place across the distant plain, I thought, then we would really have achieved something, not only for ourselves, but also for the world.

Over the years, I've walked slowly towards those shimmering trees. They are still distant. But I know I'm closer, and I'm still walking. Today my dream has changed. It is to conduct playback in a specially designed "theatre house" located in a park or forest, with people who are there for at least half a day. We will all eat a good meal together, and then we will do playback.

At this point I am less interested in the standard performance context—a one and a half hour show in a small theatre—because I feel that more often than not, the right conditions do not exist for deep stories. Rich stories, yes, but not deep ones.

But what, exactly, is a deep story? For me, a deep story is a story that is first and foremost of vital importance to the teller. It is the kind of story that creates a hush in the hall because everyone is listening so intently. A deep story is fundamentally a story where the sense of risk is palpable—the teller's risk of daring to tell or getting it clear; the actors' risk in trying to get it right; and the risk that certain members of the audience will not be able to bear it. These are the core stories, of a child's death, of violent attack, of grave social injustice, life's nightmares. They are not all tragic, certainly—a deep story may be gloriously happy. Whatever it is about, however, when faced with a deep story, we feel the soul of the teller hovering in the room. The teller becomes acutely vulnerable, which gives actors and audience a great power. There can be no neutral outcome.

We can distinguish a deep story in this sense from a rich story, one that may be everyday in its nature but is nonetheless full of possibilities for the performers. A rich story is the kind of story that makes possible the holographic power of playback, when a story about eating breakfast or seeing a swan is enacted so beautifully that we get a sense of the whole—the whole life of the teller, and vicariously, the whole of life.

Ideally, of course, the paths of the rich story and the deep story meet. And ideally, any story told under any circumstance—that is, no matter how anecdotal-seeming—can be rendered in such a way that we all experience it as belonging on that joined path. Such is the power of playback theatre, to lift the ordinary experience of an ordinary person to universal significance.

We may believe in playback that any story, once enacted, can be both rich and deep. It is a lofty goal. As a number of the chapters in *Gathering Voices* illustrate, it takes years to develop the listening skills to create rich stories, and considerable artistic skill. Rising to the challenge of deep stories, however, requires all that is needed for rich stories and more. The skills need to be sharper, knowledge of life greater, and most important, the performers need a kind of ritual strength.

Why are deep stories so rarely told? The interview with Uschi Sperling in these pages, "Emerging from Silence," gives us a sense—because tellers fear the negative consequences inherent in them. The teller may open her-

or himself to a pain that cannot be assuaged. The story may be too much for the actors, who will lose hold of the process. The story may be too much for the audience, causing it to reject the teller and the performance.

When we invite deep stories, our hearts may feel like breaking. It takes strength, even to watch. Our own world-view may get shaken. Handled well, the event will become what Richard Schechner calls transformational (not just transportational, the goal of conventional theatre).[1] Many people in modern society are alienated, without a place to tell their story. Playback theatre can offer that space. As they listen to the story, the attention of the witnesses crystallizes the teller's identity, and community bonds are formed.

One good aspect of modernity is that there has been a growing acceptance of universal human rights. It has become even more important to listen to one another, especially to those different from us. And if you, like me, come from a privileged background, it is especially important to listen to the *everyday* experiences of violence, class oppression, racism, sexism, and other forms of prejudice that we can hardly imagine. In this way our empathy broadens beyond our kind.

Furthermore, I believe that the forces for whitewashing history are very strong—often the rich and powerful write it to their advantage—and that therefore it is necessary to make a place for the "unofficial history" of those who suffer and are not heard. Each of our countries has secrets of the past that color our present and narrow our future. I believe playback theatre, by showing the secrets boldly, may be able to help redeem "history."

Sometimes groups are pressured to bend the playback form to become solution-oriented like Boal's Forum Theatre. Of course, there is a place for such approaches. But I am convinced there is also a place for drama that helps create the kind of dialogue that must take place prior to a search for solutions. Such dialogue, as the scientist and philosopher David Bohm points out, allows us to be in touch with what he calls the "tacit knowledge" that all of us as human beings possess. Bohm claims such interaction is the *prerequisite* for creating solutions to our many problems. I believe the ritual of playback theatre, which propels citizens to leap beyond their normal boundaries, is a wonderful contemporary way to achieve dialogue.[2]

The following conditions may be necessary for deep stories to emerge in playback theatre—workshops that are not too big or too brief, where there is a place for difference, and where attention is paid to creating an aesthetic environment. Further innovations are waiting to be discovered as we begin to understand more about the nature of playback's dramatic ritual.

I believe research and writing, such as the efforts in this volume, are important, especially since the PT process is so marvelously complex.

We have far to go. But this sense of being halfway should not diminish the importance of our journey, since it reaches towards fulfilling what may be playback's most important function—not only to voice, but to embody those aspects of our collective experience that others hide. In so doing, we make it clear to the world that we dare to lift the stones from our hearts and behold the gates of joy.

Notes

[1] See Richard Schechner, *Between Theater and Anthropology* (Philadelphia: University of Pennsylvania Press, 1985), chapter three.

[2] See David Bohm, *On Dialogue* (London: Routledge, 1996).

ABOUT THE AUTHORS

Marlies Arping, born in Germany, is a psychologist and psychodramatist. **Daniel Feldhendler** was born in France and works as a university lecturer, trainer, and psychodramatist. Graduates of the School of Playback Theatre, Marlies and Daniel have been active in playback since 1988 and founded Spiegelbühne Frankfurt in 1993.

Heinrich Dauber, Ph.D., is University Professor in the Department of Education at the University of Kassel. Since 1997 he has co-led two Kassel playback groups with his wife Charlette Auque-Dauber. Recent books include *The Project was Successful... Story of an Encounter between German and Zimbabwean Teachers and Students* (IKO 1998), and *Preparing a School Practicum: Pedagogical Perspectives* (Klinkhardt 1998).

Fe Day lives in Auckland, Aotearoa/New Zealand, where she works as a storyteller, teacher, and facilitator. Introduced to playback theatre in 1982, Fe was part of Auckland Playback Theatre for twelve years. As a learning support lecturer at Auckland Institute of Technology, she is involved in exploring the connections between action methods, social change, and education.

Jonathan Fox now directs the School of Playback Theatre at Vassar College in New York State. He is the former artistic director of the original playback theatre company, founded in 1975. In addition to his work teaching playback around the world, he is a psychodramatist and a storyteller. Jonathan is the author of *Acts of Service* (Tusitala Publishing 1994) and the editor of *The Essential Moreno* (Springer 1987).

Folma Hoesch, Ph.D., was born in northern Germany and has been living in Switzerland since 1964. Originally a teacher of German literature and history, she draws on process-oriented psychology, psychodrama, and playback theatre in her work at the college level and in private practice with individuals and groups.

Tarquam McKenna is a drama lecturer at Edith Cowan University in Perth, Australia. An actor with Perth Playback since 1989, he also teaches playback, seeing it as an occasion to give voice to the unspoken experiences of community. His current Ph.D. research addresses identity and belonging for gay and lesbian people in education.

József Parádi, M.D., of Budapest, Hungary is a psychotherapist and has been working with dreams for five years. He is a member of Budapest Improvisation Theater and serves on the Board of the International Playback Theatre Network (IPTN).

Jo Salas is a co-founder of playback theatre and the author of *Improvising Real Life: Personal Story in Playback Theatre* (Tusitala Publishing 1993), also in German and Japanese translations. She is the director of Hudson River Playback Theatre and teaches playback internationally.

András Zánkay is a clinical psychologist, a psychodrama T.E.P. of the Hungarian Psychodrama Association, a playback actor in Rogtonzesek Szinhaza Company in Budapest since 1992, and leader and conductor of Playback Theatre Pecs since 1995.

APPENDIX A

PROGRAM OF THE SYMPOSIUM
ON PLAYBACK THEATRE
Gesamthochschule Kassel (Kassel University), May 16-18, 1997

~ FRIDAY, MAY 16 ~

Heinrich Dauber, Ph.D., Kassel, *Germany*
Tracing the Songlines—auf der Suche nach den Quellen des Playback Theaters

Linda M. Park-Fuller, Ph.D., Springfield, MO, USA
Re-Valuing the Oral Tradition in Higher Education: PT in the Academy

Anna Chesner, München, Germany
Dramatherapie, Psychodrama und PT:
drei dramatische Modalitäten in der Gruppentherapie

András Zánkay, Pecs, Hungary
Psychological Analysis of Interpersonal and Intrapsychic Processes,
Making Playback Effective

Hans Joss, Ph.D., Bern, Switzerland
Warum und wie wirkt Playback?

~ SATURDAY, MAY 17 ~

Jo Salas, New Paltz, NY, USA
What is "Good" Playback Theatre?

Ingeborg Vonholt, Hannover, Germany
Playback Theater—Die Bedeutung des PT als Medium der interkulturellen
Kommunikation

József Parádi, M.D., Budapest, Hungary
Playback Work with Dreams

Deborah Pearson, Perth, Australia
Playback Theatre—A Vehicle for Social Intervention

Folma Hoesch, Ph.D., Zürich, Switzerland,
Geschichtenerzählen als Prozess

Marlies Arping & Daniel Feldhendler, Frankfurt, Germany
Praxisaspekte aus dem Leben einer PT Gruppe

Tarquam McKenna, Perth, Australia
Layers of Meaning—Research and Playback Theatre: A Soulful Construct

Sunday, May 18

Jean-Pierre Klein, M.D., Paris, France
L'auteur examine les raisons de l'effect thérapeutique du Playback sur le conteur

Fe Day, Auckland, New Zealand
How do I know who/where I am until I hear what I say?

Synne Platander, Stockholm, Sweden
In Search of Encounter—the Playback Approach

Asha Richard, Obertshausen, Germany
Rituale, Räume, Zwischenräume, Dauer im PT

To obtain texts of the presentations please contact:

Fachbereich I
Gesamthochschule Kassel
Nora-Platielstr. 1
34127 Kassel, Germany
Fax: 49 561 804 3043

APPENDIX B

PLAYBACK THEATRE RESOURCES

The **International Playback Theatre Network** is a support organization for playback theatre performers and teachers. INTERPLAY, the IPTN's newsletter, is published three times a year. The IPTN is registered as a not-for-profit corporation under the name Playback Theater, Inc.

There are currently IPTN members in the following countries: Argentina, Australia, Austria, Belize, Brazil, Canada, Denmark, England, Fiji Islands, Finland, France, Germany, Hong Kong, Hungary, Israel, Italy, Japan, Northern Ireland, Nepal, Netherlands, New Zealand, Pakistan, Scotland, Sweden, Switzerland, United States.

Practitioner and group members of the IPTN are entitled to use both the name and the logo.

For information about the IPTN, please contact:
IPTN
PO Box 1173
New Paltz, NY 12561 USA
www.playbacknet.org/iptn

Founded in 1993, the **School of Playback Theatre** offers a comprehensive training designed to meet the wide variety of needs, interests, and goals of playback leaders and practitioners.

Every July, a sequence of playback courses is held at Vassar College in Poughkeepsie, New York, including the five-day foundation Core Training, four and five-day Selected Topic courses, the two-week PT Practice and the three-week PT Leadership, culminating with graduation.

School courses are also held in Japan, Germany, England, and other locations.

For information, please contact:

School of Playback Theatre
Jonathan Fox, Director
137 Hasbrouck Road
New Paltz, NY 12561 USA
Tel: 914 255-8163 Fax: 914 255-1281
www.playbacknet.org/school

INDEX

AVAILABLE FROM Tusitala Publishing

Books

Improvising Real Life: Personal Story in Playback Theatre by Jo Salas (1993) ISBN 0-9642350-1-3

> *"This is a must-read book not only for theatre artists, but for educators and social service professionals interested in the arts as a tool toward both self-expression and community building."*
> —Mady Schutzman, Co-Editor, *Playing Boal: Theatre, Therapy, Activism*

Acts of Service: Spontaneity, Commitment, Tradition in the Nonscripted Theatre by Jonathan Fox (1994) ISBN 0-9642350-0-5

> *"Jonathan Fox's description of the parallel paths of scripted and nonscripted theatre is seminal."*
> —Joel Plotkin, State University of New York

Music

Listen and Remember: 23 songs for groups, Jo Salas and Friends (available on CD and cassette with lyric booklet)

> *"Uplifting, cheerful and perfect for group participation."*
> —Artie Traum, guitarist and recording artist

Circus Decisions, 11 original songs, Jo Salas (available on CD and cassette)

> *"Melodic originality, versatility of mood, and lyrical literacy."*
> —Woodstock Times

To order, please contact:

Tusitala Publishing
137 Hasbrouck Road
New Paltz, NY 12561 USA
Fax: 914 255-1281
www.playbacknet.org/tusitala